A Study on Cross-Linguistic Variations
in Realization Patterns:
New Proposals Based on Competition Theory

A Study on Cross-Linguistic Variations in Realization Patterns:

New Proposals Based on Competition Theory

Kazuya Nishimaki

KAITAKUSHA

Kaitakusha Co., Ltd.
5-2, Mukogaoka 1-chome
Bunkyo-ku, Tokyo 113-0023
Japan

A Study on Cross-Linguistic Variations in Realization Patterns:
New Proposals Based on Competition Theory

Published in Japan
by Kaitakusha Co., Ltd., Tokyo

Copyright © 2018
by Kazuya Nishimaki

All rights reserved. No part of this publication may be
reproduced, stored in a retrieval system, or transmitted,
in any form or by any means, electronic, mechanical,
photocopying, recording, or otherwise, without the prior
permission of the copyright owner.

First published 2018

Printed and bound in Japan
by Hinode Printing Co., Ltd.

Cover design by Shihoko Nakamura

Acknowledgments

This book is a revised version of my doctoral dissertation accepted by the University of Tsukuba in January 2016. Eight years ago, Yukio Hirose allowed me to study at the University of Tsukuba. Then, six years ago, Masaharu Shimada and Akiko Nagano told me that Competition Theory was a worthwhile subject to pursue in my doctoral dissertation. Since then, this theory has been the main topic of my research. This thesis is the result of my research on Competition Theory over the past several years. I could not have continued my studies and completed this thesis without supports from many people. Here, I would like to thank them all. First of all, I would like to express my deep gratitude to Masaharu Shimada, Yukio Hirose, and Akiko Nagano.

Masaharu Shimada, my principal academic advisor, has been both strict and kind while training me as a linguist. He always works together with his students to determine problems and to discover solutions to those problems. He was the first person to introduce me to the philosophy of linguistics and the realities of academic research. He is a strict generative theorist and under his tutelage, I realized that a formal approach to language can be fascinating. He has always advised me that I should behave reasonably in my everyday life because everything that I do in daily life affects my academic life and research. In this sense, he has also trained me to be a full-fledged member of society. No matter how busy he has been, he has always taken the time to repeatedly revise the papers I have submitted to conferences or journals, correcting my errors. I am a slow learner, but he has led me in the right direction on every occasion.

Yukio Hirose, my committee's chief, has taken care of me since I began my academic career at the University of Tsukuba, encouraging me whenever I have had trouble. Due to his keen insight into English and the whole area of linguistics, his comments in classes were very informative for me. Although he is not a morphologist, he is one among those who understand my morphological studies the best. When I asked him to read earlier drafts of this thesis, he told me that Competition Theory was interesting to researchers other than morphologists as well, assuring me that my studies had broader applications.

Akiko Nagano, a member of my committee, established a foundation for my morphological studies. It was not until I attended her lectures at the University of Tsukuba that I received careful training in morphology. Before that, I had only read a few introductory morphology books. In her classes, I learned about my own lack of knowledge and misunderstandings of the topic. I owe my morphological background to her teaching.

My thanks also go to Nobuhiro Kaga and Naoaki Wada, the other members of my committee. They carefully read an earlier version of this thesis. From a derivational-theoretic point of view, Nobuhiro Kaga gave me thought-provoking comments and suggestions. Naoaki Wada made me open my eyes to semanticopragmatic aspects of morphosyntactic phenomena. What they pointed out helped me develop the ideas in this thesis. And they greatly encouraged me to finish my dissertation.

In addition to my thesis committee members, I am indebted to many faculty and staff members at the University of Tsukuba, including Masaru Kanetani, Yuichi Ono, and Shuto Yamamura. I also wish to thank the following people within Tsukuba: Suguru Mikami, Tetsuya Kogusuri, Shun Kudo, Akihiko Sakamoto, Masaki Yasuhara, Tatsuhiro Okubo, Keita Ikarashi, Shotaro Namiki, Ryohei Naya, and Masatoshi Honda. The discussions and joint works I have conducted with these people have contributed to developing my research. In particular, I owe Chapter 4, Section 4.3 and Section 4.4 to Keita Ikarashi and Masaki Yasuhara, respectively. Furthermore, I should express my thanks to my colleagues at ToTo motors Co. Ltd, where I worked for nine years after I graduated from Aoyama Gakuin University in 1999. They all encouraged me to fulfil my goal when I quitted my job to return to

Aoyama Gakuin University as a graduate student.

Last but not least, I am very grateful to Minoji Akimoto, Kazuo Nakazawa, and Makoto Ichikawa, who took care of me at Aoyama Gakuin University. Minoji Akimoto told me about the existence of the research area of 'English linguistics,' when I was an undergraduate student at Aoyama Gakuin University. His lectures motivated me to study English linguistics. Kazuo Nakazawa was my academic adviser at Aoyama Gakuin University. He told me that behind trivial facts there lurk interesting phenomena. His insightful analysis always fascinated and inspired me. And I owe him a great deal for my English literacy. Makoto Ichikawa, now an assistant professor of Tokyo University of Science, has been a friend of mine since 2008, when I returned to Aoyama Gakuin University as a graduate student. We have since gotten along with each other because, coincidentally, we are of the same age and share similar backgrounds. For this reason, he has always given me useful advice as a Ph.D. holder as well as a researcher.

Kazuya Nishimaki
October 2018

Contents

Acknowledgments .... **v**

Chapter 1   Introduction **1**
   1.1. Aim and Scope 1
   1.2. Organization 5

Chapter 2   The General Architecture of Competition Theory **9**
   2.1. Introduction 9
   2.2. Competition Theory in the Representational Modularity Model 10
   2.3. The Basic Framework of Competition Theory 14
      2.3.1. Mechanism of Morphology-Syntax Competition 14
      2.3.2. Language Types: Morphology-Preferring and Syntax-Preferring
           Languages 17
   2.4. Competition-Theoretic View of Compounding and its Consequences ... 18
      2.4.1. English 'Root Compounds' as Lexicalized Phrases 18
      2.4.2. Structural Analysis of Synthetic Compounds 20
   2.5. Main Claim: Clustering Effects of a Single Macroparameter 23
   2.6. Theoretical Background: Approach Based on Optimality Theory ... 26

2.7. Summary ⋯⋯⋯⋯⋯⋯⋯⋯⋯⋯⋯⋯⋯⋯⋯⋯⋯⋯⋯⋯⋯⋯⋯⋯ 31

Chapter 3 Realization Patterns of Nominal Modification in English and Japanese ⋯⋯⋯⋯⋯⋯⋯⋯⋯⋯⋯⋯⋯⋯⋯⋯⋯⋯⋯ 33

3.1. Introduction ⋯⋯⋯⋯⋯⋯⋯⋯⋯⋯⋯⋯⋯⋯⋯⋯⋯⋯⋯⋯⋯⋯ 33

3.2. Baker (2003a, b): Cross-Linguistic Variations in Attested Types of Nominal Modification ⋯⋯⋯⋯⋯⋯⋯⋯⋯⋯⋯⋯⋯⋯⋯⋯ 35

3.2.1. Two Types of Nominal Modification: Direct and Indirect Modification ⋯⋯⋯⋯⋯⋯⋯⋯⋯⋯⋯⋯⋯⋯⋯⋯⋯⋯ 35

3.2.2. Direct Modification as an Adjectival Property ⋯⋯⋯⋯⋯ 37

3.3. Competition-Theoretic Analysis of Direct Modification ⋯⋯⋯⋯ 39

3.3.1. Japanese A-N Compounds as Morphologically-Realized Forms of Direct Modification ⋯⋯⋯⋯⋯⋯⋯⋯⋯⋯ 39

3.3.2. Diversity of Nominal Modifications in Germanic Languages ⋯ 46

3.4. Competition-Theoretic Predictions in Non-competing Circumstances 49

3.4.1. Morphologically-Realized Forms in English ⋯⋯⋯⋯⋯ 49

3.4.2. Syntactically-Realized Forms in Japanese ⋯⋯⋯⋯⋯ 50

3.5. Summary ⋯⋯⋯⋯⋯⋯⋯⋯⋯⋯⋯⋯⋯⋯⋯⋯⋯⋯⋯⋯⋯⋯⋯ 55

Chapter 4 Further Applications ⋯⋯⋯⋯⋯⋯⋯⋯⋯⋯⋯⋯⋯⋯⋯ 57

4.1. Introduction ⋯⋯⋯⋯⋯⋯⋯⋯⋯⋯⋯⋯⋯⋯⋯⋯⋯⋯⋯⋯⋯⋯ 57

4.2. Phrasal Realization vs. Compound Realization ⋯⋯⋯⋯⋯⋯ 58

4.2.1. VPs vs. V-V Compounds ⋯⋯⋯⋯⋯⋯⋯⋯⋯⋯⋯⋯⋯ 58

4.2.2. Coordinated Structure ⋯⋯⋯⋯⋯⋯⋯⋯⋯⋯⋯⋯⋯ 71

4.3. Free Forms vs. Bound Forms: Realization Patterns of Discourse Markers ⋯⋯⋯⋯⋯⋯⋯⋯⋯⋯⋯⋯⋯⋯⋯⋯⋯⋯⋯⋯⋯ 82

4.4. Conflation vs. Incorporation ⋯⋯⋯⋯⋯⋯⋯⋯⋯⋯⋯⋯⋯ 92

4.4.1. The Distinction between Conflating and Incorporating Languages 93

4.4.2. Competition-Theoretic Analysis of Conflation and Incorporation 97

4.4.3. Simplex Forms vs. Complex Forms ⋯⋯⋯⋯⋯⋯⋯⋯ 102

4.5. Summary ⋯⋯⋯⋯⋯⋯⋯⋯⋯⋯⋯⋯⋯⋯⋯⋯⋯⋯⋯⋯⋯⋯ 115

Chapter 5 Conclusion ⋯⋯⋯⋯⋯⋯⋯⋯⋯⋯⋯⋯⋯⋯⋯⋯⋯⋯ 117

Appendix   Lexicalization Analysis of English 'Root Compounds' and
            Related Issues ··· **123**
1. Introduction ·· 123
2. The Definition of Lexicalization and Compounding: Their
   Fundamental Difference ··· 124
3. Lexicalization Analysis of English 'Root Compounds' ···················· 127
   3.1. Non-uniformity of N-N and A-N 'Root Compounds' ·············· 127
   3.2. Other Cases of Lexicalized Phrases ······································· 132
4. Verbal N-N Combinations as Attributive Phrases ·························· 137
5. Lexicalization as a Language-Neutral Process and Cross-Linguistic
   Variations ·· 142
6. Summary ··· 144

References ·· **147**

Index ·· **163**

Chapter 1

Introduction

1.1. Aim and Scope

Chomsky (1965: 27–28) defines the primary concern of linguistic theory as follows:

> (1) Consequently, the main task of linguistic theory must be to develop an account of linguistic universals that, on the one hand, will not be falsified by the actual diversity of languages [...]

Tackling this task, Ackema and Neeleman (2001, 2004, 2005, 2007, 2010) propose a theory that hypothesizes that an unmarked realization form of a structure is parameterized in terms of either morphology or syntax, depending on which is more prominent in a given language. Since the notion of competition between the two grammatical modules plays a crucial role in this theory, we call it Competition Theory. Within the framework of this theory, the present thesis makes cross-linguistic comparison to explore its theoretical possibilities. There are a few works adopting Competition Theory. For example, Kechagias (2005) makes a competition-theoretic analysis of compounds in Modern Greek; and, Nagano (2013) applies the relevant theory to the analysis of attributive modifiers in English and Romance languages. Nevertheless, there has been no comprehensive cross-linguistic research based on

Competition Theory. Therefore, it remains unclear what aspects of language this theory sheds new light on or how it does so. The aim of the present thesis is to contribute to developing a competition-theoretic approach and to demonstrate its promise in presenting a new perspective on cross-linguistic variations and unifying otherwise separately-treated phenomena. Our enterprise is the first comprehensive study of comparative syntax based on Competition Theory.

Ackema and Neeleman (2001, 2004, 2005, 2007, 2010) mainly apply Competition Theory to data concerning a realization pattern of a predicate-argument structure (or head-complement structure) with special reference to Germanic languages. Given that it is a general theory, we reasonably assume that it should hold true for other types of structures and capture variations among typologically unrelated languages. Based on this assumption, the present thesis analyzes the realization patterns of a modifiee-modifier structure, another asymmetrical head-nonhead structure, in two typologically unrelated languages: English and Japanese. Specifically, we examine contrastive realization patterns of nominal modification, which are illustrated in the following translation pair (quoted from *Kenkyusha's New Japanese-English Dictionary* (henceforth, Kenkyusha's Dictionary)):

(2) a. an <u>old</u> family   (intended reading: an ancient family)
  b. <u>kyuu</u>-ka
   ancient-family
   'an old family'

       (Kenkyusha's Dictionary, s.v. *kyuu-ka* 'old family')

The Japanese counterparts of the adjective *old* and the noun *family* in (2a) are *kyuu-* and *-ka*, respectively, in the intended reading, as shown in (2b).[1] The difference in realization patterns is noteworthy. The English *old family* in (2a) is a phrase because it can be syntactically divided (e.g. *an <u>old</u> illustrious family* (Kenkyusha's Dictionary, s.v. *kyuu-ka* 'old family')). This English nominal phrase is translated into the Japanese A-N compound *kyuu-ka*, as

---

[1] Note that *kyuu-* 'old' and *-ka* 'family' are not affixes, though they are bound morphemes. According to Kageyama (1993: 13–14), if bound morphemes can occur both before and after other elements (e.g. *sin-<u>kyuu</u>(-no)* 'new and old' and <u>ka</u>-*zoku* 'family'), they make up compounds. Also, Lieber and Štekauer (2009: 4–5) suggest that the elements that make up compounds in some languages are bound morphemes.

shown in (2b). Its compoundhood is corroborated by its syntactic opacity (e.g. *kyuu-(*yuisyoaru)-ka* 'an old illustrious family'), i.e. the defining property of words, which is known as the Lexical Integrity Principle (LIP) (see Lapointe (1980: 8); Di Sciullo and Williams (1987: 49); Bresnan and Mchombo (1995: 51)). It is thus possible to consider that the same structure of nominal modification is realized as a phrase in English but as a word in Japanese. Within the framework of Competition Theory, we claim that this contrast comes from a parametric distinction between English and Japanese.

Here, we would like to explicate general guidelines for our research. The first and most important guideline is that as a generative enterprise our cross-linguistic research follows the Uniformity Principle, which is formulated in (3).

(3)   In the absence of compelling evidence to the contrary, assume languages to be uniform, with variety restricted to easily detectable properties of utterances.   (Chomsky (2001b: 2))

In this respect, cross-linguistic comparison in generative grammar differs fundamentally from functionalist typology, which takes it for granted that "languages can differ from each other without limit and in unpredicted ways (Joos (1957: 96))." This principle implies that cross-linguistic variations lie in externalization. Chomsky (2010: 60) states this point as follows:

(4)   Parametrization and diversity too would be mostly- maybe entirely-restricted to externalization. Though it is contested, that may include linearization, which appears to play no role in syntax and the C-I interface, and the options for linearization.

Second, the present thesis intends to use the term 'construction' merely for descriptive taxonomy, assuming that we do not have constructions specific to a particular component (syntax or morphology) or those specific to a particular language (e.g. English and Japanese). This treatment is based on the abandonment of the notion of construction in the Principles-and-Parameters approach and the Minimalist Program (cf. Goldberg (1995); Croft (2001)). For example, Chomsky (1995: 25) states that "[t]he notion of construction, in the traditional sense, effectively disappears; it is perhaps useful for descriptive taxonomy but has no theoretical status."

Finally, following Baker (1996, 2008), Snyder (1995, 2001, 2012), and

Ackema and Neeleman (2004), we believe in the existence of macroparameters as core principles of grammar; and we assume that they should thus be distinguished from microparameters. Baker (2008: 355–358) distinguishes between these two types of parameters as follows. Macroparameters are hardwired into the syntax itself with large-scale consequences, typically visible in typologically unrelated languages, whereas microparameters have limited consequences that result from features being associated with specific lexical items, typically visible in closely related languages (cf. Borer (1984); Chomsky (1995)). Competition Theory postulates a macroparameter that determines an unmarked realization pattern in a given language in terms of either morphology or syntax.

According to Baker (2010), cross-linguistic comparison in generative grammar must seek to answer the following questions:

(5) a. What properties of natural human languages are genuinely universal, inherent to the human species as such?

b. What properties of natural human languages vary from one human language to another?

c. Which aspects of variation are patterned, systematic, and grammatical in nature, and which aspects of variation are random, idiosyncratic, and lexical in nature?

(Baker (2010: 286))

Our analysis in the succeeding chapters shows that cross-linguistic comparison based on Competition Theory can answer these questions as in (6).

(6) a. Principles or constrains are genuinely universal, inherent to the human species as such.

b. Realization forms of underlying morphosyntactic structures vary from one human language to another.

c. Selection of a particular type of realization form in a particular language is patterned, systematic, and grammatical in nature, and actual tokens of the selected type are random, idiosyncratic, and lexical in nature.

1.2. Organization

The organization of this thesis is as follows. Chapter 2 presents the general architecture of Competition Theory. This chapter mainly discusses two topics. One is how a competition-theoretic approach successfully captures the interrelation between issues concerning inter-modularity and cross-linguistic variations. The other is a competition-theoretic view of compounding, according to which the process is a parameterized option for structural realization. We consider consequences of this view with special reference to English compounds.

Chapter 3 provides a competition-theoretic analysis of the contrasting realization patterns of nominal modification between English and Japanese, as mentioned in the previous section. This analysis reveals that their contrast ultimately derives from the macroparametric distinction between English and Japanese.

Chapter 4 pursues further possibilities of Competition Theory to extend our analysis into phenomena other than nominal modification. Let us take a brief look at some examples to be dealt with in this chapter. The following translation pair involves resultative constructions:

(7) a. Hanako <u>pounded</u> the metal <u>flat</u>.   (Hasegawa (1999: 178))

   b. Hanako-ga   kinzoku-o (taira-ni) <u>tataki-nobasi-ta</u>.

      Hanako-Nom metal-Acc (flat)   pound-spread-Past

      'Hanako pounded the metal flat.'

               (Hasegawa (1999: 184), with slight modifications)

As with nominal modification, English and Japanese select a phrasal and a compound form, respectively. In (7a), the verb *to pound*, the object noun *metal*, and the adjective *flat* together form a VP which is interpreted as a resultative construction. This VP can be translated into the Japanese V-V compound *tataki-nobasu* in (7b), where the left-hand verb *tataku* corresponds to the verb *to pound* in (7a) and the right-hand verb *nobasu* 'to spread' to the adjective *flat* in (7a). As expected from the LIP, the Japanese V-V compound disallows an intervening object noun in contrast to its English phrasal counterpart (e.g. *tataki-(*kinzoku-o)-nobasu* 'to pound the metal flat'). Given these considerations, it may be safely assumed that an English VP and a Japanese

V-V compound are different forms realizing the same accomplishment of eventuality.

Nominal modification and resultative constructions concern headed structures. Let us turn from these asymmetrical structures to coordinated structures. The following translation pair indicates that English and Japanese realize a coordinated structure in the same way that they realize asymmetrical structures:

(8) a. The husband and wife cheered each other up.

b. Huu-hu-wa   tagai-o   hagemasi-ta.
   husband-wife-Top each.other-Acc cheer.up-Past
   'The husband and wife cheered each other up.'

(Kageyama (2009: 515))

In (8a), the two nouns *husband* and *wife* form a coordinated phrase with the conjunct *and*. (8b) shows that the Japanese equivalents of the English nouns *husband* and *wife* are *huu-* and *-hu*, respectively, in the intended reading. While they are in a coordinated relationship, these Japanese equivalents make up a compound without a conjunct.

Even at the discourse level, English and Japanese have contrastive realization patterns. Observe the following difference in discourse markers:

(9) a. I tell you, he is an idiot.   (Stubbs (1983: 157))

b. Ame-da yo. 'It is raining, I tell you.'   (Hirose (1995: 227))

In (9a), the sequence *I tell you* encodes a speech act of conveying some information to the addressee. In the literature, it has been pointed out that *I tell you* roughly corresponds to the bound morpheme *yo* in Japanese, as shown in the translation in (9b). In this case, we assume that the contrast between English and Japanese involves the distinction between free and bound forms.

So far, we have been concerned with contrasts in realization forms. The contrast between English and Japanese may also be found in operations. As is well known, in English, a process of conversion, which shifts categories without morphological marking (see Bauer (1983: 32)), is very productively used for word formation. For example, the conversion of nouns to verbs derives the following unergative verbs:

Chapter 1 Introduction 7

(10) belch, burp, cough, crawl, cry, dance, gallop, gleam, glitter, glow, hop, jump, laugh, leap, limp, nap, run, scream, shout, skip, sleep, sneeze, sob, somersault, sparkle, speak, stagger, sweat, talk, trot, twinkle, walk, yell   (Hale and Keyser (2002: 14))

In the literature, it is proposed that this word formation process involves the type of head movement known as conflation. On the other hand, in Japanese, a process of conversion is said to be very rare. Instead, Japanese widely uses another type of head movement, known as incorporation, for word formation. For example, it is assumed that noun incorporation derives the Japanese counterparts of English unergative verbs, e.g. *sanpo-suru* 'lit. to walk-do = to walk.' Based on these facts, it is pointed out that there is a typological difference in head movement. We demonstrate that this typological difference is reducible to a macroparametric distinction assumed under Competition Theory.

In Competition Theory, these contrasts are parallel to those observed in nominal modification and they can be accounted for in essentially the same way. Our inquiry in Chapter 4 demonstrates that a competition-theoretic approach works well for capturing cross-constructional as well as cross-linguistic variations.

Chapter 5 concludes this thesis with a summary of the claims and an outlook for our future research.

Chapter 2

The General Architecture of Competition Theory

2.1. Introduction

This chapter presents the general architecture of Competition Theory. In (generative) linguistics, 'competition' has been a familiar phenomenon. In the literature, it has been observed that if two forms compete for a certain expression, a more specific form wins the competition and blocks the occurrence of a more general form. This observation is generalized as the Elsewhere Condition by Kiparsky (1982). Poser (1992) observes that lexical comparatives block the occurrence of phrasal ones in English:

(1) a. bigger   a′. *more big
    b. *symmetricer   b′. more symmetric

(Poser (1992: 122))

Based on this blocking phenomenon, called Poser blocking, Poser points out that morphology and syntax compete with each other. In terms of the Elsewhere Condition, Poser blocking means that lexical comparatives are more marked than phrasal ones: the former are based exhaustively on (phonologically) shorter adjectives and the latter are available elsewhere. Competition Theory also considers morphology and syntax to be in a competing relationship. However, this theory is fundamentally different from that of

Poser (1992) in assuming that the (un)markedness of competing forms is evaluated on the basis of language-specific preference. Elaborating on this point, this chapter explores how morphology and syntax compete within the framework of Competition Theory

The organization of this chapter is as follows. Ackema and Neeleman (2004) propose Competition Theory as part of their own model of grammar, and Section 2.2 considers how Competition Theory is organized into this model. Section 2.3 reviews the basic framework of Competition Theory, which is due to Ackema and Neeleman. Section 2.4 moves on to discuss a competition-theoretic view of compounding. Competition Theory assumes that this process is a parameterized option for structural realization; it can be used as a default option in some languages but not in others, and English is grouped into a language where it is not available as a default option. We examine consequences of this assumption for the analysis of compounds in English. Section 2.5 explicates the main claim of the present thesis by observing what phenomena can be nicely captured within the framework of Competition Theory. For a better understanding of Competition Theory, Section 2.6 touches on its theoretical background. We consider what kind of approach it adopts as a generative model.

2.2. Competition Theory in the Representational Modularity Model

Ackema and Neeleman (2004) build a model of grammar, on the basis of Representational Modularity (see Jackendoff (1997b)). For convenience, we refer to this model as the Representational Modularity Model. Representational Modularity states that phonology, semantics, and syntax are independent generative systems associated by mapping principles and that the well-formedness of a given expression is determined by the interaction of these independent systems. The morphology-syntax competition postulated in Competition Theory is an instantiation of this interaction.

The Representational Modularity Model consists of the modules listed in Table 1, which are schematized as in Figure 1.

Chapter 2　The General Architecture of Competition Theory　11

Table 1　Grammatical Modules

	Modules	Functions
(a)	LEXICON	listing
(b)	SYNTAX	hierarchical representation (structure building)
(b′)	syntax (Phrasal Syntax)	phrasal-level hierarchical representation
(b″)	morphology (Word Syntax)	word-level hierarchical representation
(c)	SEMANTICS	semantic representation
(d)	PHONOLOGY	phonological representation
(e)	PF	structural realization (morphophonological shape)

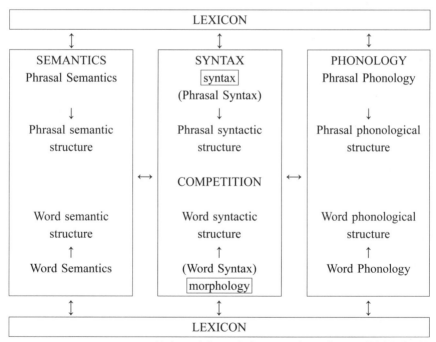

(Adapted from Ackema and Neeleman (2004: 277))

Figure 1　The Representational Modularity Model

The basic picture of this model is as follows. On the traditional view since Bloomfield (1933), the lexicon (Table 1 (a)) is defined as "a list of syntactic, morphological and phonological irregularities (Ackema and Neeleman (2004: 50))." This module supplies lexical items to SYNTAX (Table (1b)), SEMANTICS (Table (1c)), and PHONOLOGY (Table (1d)). They are independent systems that generate their own representations (i.e. syntactic, semantic, and phonological representations), which are related with each other by mapping principles (in Figure 1, '↔' and '↕' indicate mapping relations). These three components each contain a submodule that generates phrasal-level representations and a submodule that generates word-level representations. According to Ackema and Neeleman's (2004) strict definition, the term 'syntax' refers to a submodule that generates phrasal-level hierarchical representations, as shown in Table 1 (b'), while the term 'morphology' refers to a submodule that generates word-level hierarchical representations, as shown in Table 1 (b''). PF (Table 1 (e)) is responsible for structural realization, providing morphosyntactic representations with morphophonological shapes. Note here that the Representational Modularity Model adopts the Separation Hypothesis (e.g. Beard (1995), Halle and Marantz (1993)). That is, phonological materials are absent in semantic and morphosyntactic representations, which are composed only of abstract feature bundles. It is not until derivation reaches PF that these feature bundles are endowed with morphophonological shapes by the operation of so-called Late Insertion (see Halle and Marantz (1993)).

The point is that morphology and syntax are on an equal footing as independent generative systems. This means that the locus of merger is underspecified and that in principle lexical items can be merged in either of the two modules. Based on this equal status, Competition Theory assumes that morphology and syntax compete for the PF realization of abstract structures and that the winner of the competition is parameterized cross-linguistically for each particular language. Thus, languages are classified as morphology-preferring and syntax-preferring, depending on the chosen value. Morphology-preferring and syntax-preferring languages choose the morphological and syntactic value, respectively. This is a core assumption of Competition Theory. One might wonder why morphology-syntax competition takes place at all or why a preferred option, either morphology or syntax, is determined for each particular language. Ackema and Neeleman (2001) suggest that this is due to computational economy. For example, the following statement explains why syntax-preferring languages are required to use syntax as much as possible and to minimize the use of morphology:

(2) Continuation in syntax implies that only one rule system will be operative. Continuation in morphology implies that in addition to the syntactic rule system, a second rule system must be activated. From a computational point of view, this procedure would seem costly, and it will therefore be avoided if possible.

(Ackema and Neeleman (2001: 31-32))

According to this statement, the use of both morphology and syntax is costly.

Now, we consider further implications of the model illustrated in Figure 1. This model implies that there are cross-linguistic variations as to merger in SYNTAX: lexical items are merged morphologically in morphology-preferring languages but syntactically in syntax-preferring languages. This means that these two types of languages have different underlying structures. Here recall our research guideline given in Chapter 1. It dictates that we should follow Chomsky's (2001b) Uniformity Principle (see (3) in Chapter 1) to assume that cross-linguistic variations lie in externalization. Given this, it is undesirable to assume that underlying structure has cross-linguistic variations. In order to ensure faithfulness to our research guideline, we would like to revise the Representational Modularity Model, as in Figure 2.

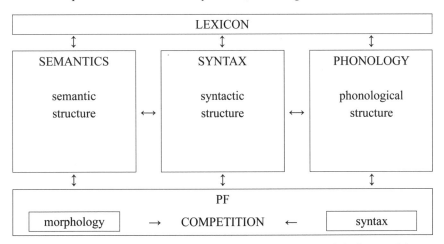

Figure 2 Revised Version of the Representational Modularity Model

In this revised version, SYNTAX is the only module that builds morphosyntactic structures, whereas morphology and syntax are responsible exhaustively for structural realization at PF (we assume that SYNTAX is equivalent to narrow syntax in the Minimalist Program). The merger of lexical items in SYNTAX involves no morphology-syntax distinction. Through this merger, morphosyntactic structures are generated. Then, in PF, morphology and syntax compete in order to realize these structures: either morphological or syntactic realization is selected, depending on the distinction between morphology-preferring and syntax-preferring languages.

To illustrate the derivation in the model given in Figure 2, let us examine comparatives in English. Following Embick and Marantz (2008), we assume that comparatives are headed by the functional category Degree. In SYNTAX, adjectives and Degree, which are taken from LEXICON, are merged to generate morphosyntactic structures like [_Deg Degree [Adjective]]. In PF, these structures can be realized as lexical comparatives in morphology or as phrasal comparatives in syntax. Suppose that English is a syntax-preferring language, as seen in the next section. Then, as a result of the morphology-syntax competition, phrasal comparatives are selected as surface forms to block lexical comparatives (e.g. *more symmetric* vs. **symmetricer*). If monosyllabic or di-syllabic adjectives are involved, lexical, but not phrasal, comparatives are required (e.g. *bigger* vs. **more big*). Given that the number of syllables counts as phonological information, we may assume that in the case of these adjectives comparatives must be realized by morphology for some phonological reason. If so, we may analyze lexical comparatives as resulting from the interaction between PHONOLOGY and morphology.

2.3. The Basic Framework of Competition Theory

2.3.1. Mechanism of Morphology-Syntax Competition

In a series of works, Ackema and Neeleman (2001, 2004, 2005, 2007, 2010) elaborate on the precise mechanism of the morphology-syntax competition. A crucial point for this mechanism is that the competition in question is at work under the conditions of structural and semantic identity, which can be formulated as follows:

(3) Conditions on Competition
  a. Structural Identity:
     Morphological and syntactic realizations are structurally identical in that the same categories are merged in both realizations.
  b. Semantic Identity:
     Morphological and syntactic realizations are semantically identical in that merged categories have the same grammatical relationship in both realizations.

Morphology and syntax compete for PF realization only if conditions (3a) and (3b) are both met. Ackema and Neeleman (2001, 2004, 2005, 2007, 2010) explain how these conditions apply by examining the PF realization of the predicate-argument relationship, and the verb-object relationship in particular. For example, the underlying syntactic structure in which *to drive* takes *truck* as its argument can be phonologically realized as either the compound form *to truck-drive* or the phrasal form *to drive trucks*.[1] In both forms, a noun and a verb are merged and these categories have the predicate-argument relationship. Therefore, the compound form and VP form meet the two conditions given in (3) and compete with each other. The fact that English uses the latter form (in most contexts) leads Ackema and Neeleman to conclude that English prefers syntax for PF realization and that the phrasal form wins the competition to block the compound form. In morphology-preferring languages, the compound form corresponding to *to truck-drive* should be selected instead. To put it differently, Competition Theory requires syntax-preferring and morphology-preferring languages to minimize the morphological and syntactic complexity, respectively, of realization forms.

The conditions given in (3a) Structural Identity and (3b) Semantic Identity tell us that the competition explored here is irrelevant to the pair of different abstract structures or different semantics. This is illustrated by the possibility of N-V compound forms like *to color-code*, where nouns and verbs have the predicate-adjunct relationship in the intended reading. These com-

---

[1] It is irrelevant to competition whether *to drive* and *truck* project prior to their merger. Ackema and Neeleman (2004: 51) explain the reason as follows:

  (i) Because a head and its (extended) projections share identifying features, such as category, competition does not distinguish between merger of the terminals α and β and merger of α with an (extended) projection of β.

pound forms can coexist with VP forms such as *to code with colors* with the same semantics, because of their different structures. For example, Ackema and Neeleman (2004: 60) analyze *to color-code* and *to code with colors* as in (4a) and (4b), respectively.

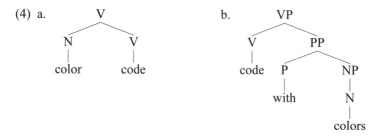

The compound form *to color-code* is the merger of a noun and verb, whereas the VP form *to code with colors* is the merger of a verb and PP. Also, the relevant compound forms are not in competition with VP forms such as *to code colors*, even though both forms result from the merger of nouns and verbs. This failure of competition is due to their different semantics: the two categories have the predicate-adjunct relationship in the compound forms but the predicate-argument relationship in the VP forms.

The morphology-syntax competition always obtains if both morphological and syntactic realizations can be candidates for a surface form of a given abstract structure. If either of the possibilities is excluded for some independent reason, however, the remaining possibility, whether a morphological or syntactic realization, must be chosen, regardless of the parametric value. Ackema and Neeleman (2001, 2004, 2005, 2007, 2010) show this by focusing on the fact that whereas English does not have the verbal compound *to truck-drive* per se, it does have the synthetic compound *truck driver*. Although *to truck-drive* is not allowed because its competitor *to drive trucks* is selected as a surface form, it is involved in the derivation of the synthetic compound *truck driver*. This means that the verbal compound form is not ungrammatical but unselected in English. According to Ackema and Neeleman, because suffixes, e.g. *-er*, require morphologically-realized objects as their bases, VP forms cannot be candidates for suffixation. Therefore, VP forms cannot compete with compound forms when word formation involves suffixes.[2] In an environment

---

[2] One might expect that inflectional suffixes have the effect of preventing competition,

where syntactic realization is not allowed, morphological realization is possible even in a syntax-preferring language such as English.

2.3.2. Language Types: Morphology-Preferring and Syntax-Preferring Languages

Next, we go on to consider how we can tell the difference between morphology-preferring and syntax-preferring languages. Ackema and Neeleman (2001, 2004, 2005, 2007, 2010) use the (un)attestedness of verbal complexes as a criterion for distinguishing between these two types of languages. Based on the unattestedness of genuine verbal compounds, for example, *to truck-drive* in English, Ackema and Neeleman (2004: Ch. 3) assume that it belongs to the group of syntax-preferring languages. Ackema and Neeleman (2004: 55, fn. 2) suggest that the same is true of nearly all Germanic languages.[3] In contrast, Ackema and Neeleman (2004: 85–88) consider polysynthetic languages to be typical examples of morphology-preferring languages. For instance, concepts typically expressed by adverbials in English must be expressed morphologically as parts of verbal complexes in Yimas, which is spoken in Papua New Guinea:

---

contrary to fact:

(i) *Mary truck-drives all day long. (Ackema and Neeleman (2004: 61))

Assuming that inflectional suffixes do not head words, Ackema and Neeleman (2004: 61) analyze the inflected structures of *to drive trucks* and *to truck-drive* as in (iia) and (iib), respectively.

(ii) a.   b.

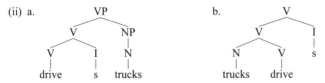

In both structures, verbs and nouns merge, which induces the morphology-syntax competition. These considerations indicate that only category-changing affixes serve to prevent competition. Therefore, prefixes, i.e. category-neutral affixes, do no suspend competition:

(iii)   Mary {re-paints the wall / *re-wall-paints} every year.

(Ackema and Neeleman (2004: 62))

[3] Observing that Frisian has genuine argumental N-V compounds, Ackema and Neeleman suggest that it may be a morphology-preferring language, which is exceptional among Germanic languages.

(5) Tpwi   i-kay-a-pan-kiak.
    sago.X.PL   X.PL.O-IPL.A-DEF-pound-NEAR.FUTURE
    'We will pound sago tomorrow.'

(Ackema and Neeleman (2004: 87))

In (5), the time adverbial *kiak* 'tomorrow' is a part of the morphological verbal complex. By the same reasoning, Japanese can be classified as a morphology-preferring language because it has expressions that involve verbal complexes, such as verbal compounds (e.g. *sen-sya(-suru)* (V-N) 'to wash cars,' *ude-gumi(-suru)* (N-V) 'to fold one's arms,' and *tabe-hazimeru* (V-V) 'to begin to eat') (see Kageyama (1993, 2009)). Thus, a particular language is assumed to be classified as syntax-preferring or morphology-preferring in Competition Theory.

2.4. Competition-Theoretic View of Compounding and its Consequences

As our discussion so far suggests, Competition Theory views compounding as an option for morphological realization. In this view, compounds can be defined as morphologically-realized forms of the merger of lexical items. In other words, Competition Theory assumes that the use of compounding is parametrically designated as a default option in morphology-preferring languages but not in syntax-preferring ones, where the merger of lexical items results in phrasal realization. Such competition-theoretic view of compounding entails some consequences for the analysis of compounds in syntax-preferring languages. This section explores these consequences with special reference to English compounds.

2.4.1. English 'Root Compounds' as Lexicalized Phrases

To begin with, we consider what the above view implies for the traditional classification of compounds. In the literature, they have been classified into synthetic and root compounds. The given view leads us to the consequence that only synthetic compounds are possible in English, namely, as a syntax-preferring language with no root compound. A crucial difference between

Chapter 2   The General Architecture of Competition Theory   19

these two types is that agentive -*er* or the gerundive -*ing* is involved in synthetic but not in root compounds (e.g. *truck driv<u>er</u>/truck driv<u>ing</u>* vs. *ballot box*) (see, for example, Bloomfield (1933); Marchand (1969); Roeper and Siegel (1978); Fabb (1984)). As seen in Section 2.3.1, synthetic compounds are allowed even in English because selectional restrictions on these suffixes prevent the morphology-syntax competition; in contrast, root compounds are impossible in English because nothing suspends this competition.

For example, let us consider the following N-N and A-N combinations, which are listed as root compounds in an English dictionary:

(6) a.   ballot box, boom box, box lunch, box number, box office, box-wood
    b.   black belt, blackberry, blackbird, blackboard, black box, black eye

(COBUILD, (a); s.v. *box*, (b); s.v. *black*)

Competition Theory states that they cannot be compounds but syntactic phrases, because the former should be in competition with and blocked by the latter. If so, a natural question is why such combinations as those given in (6) exhibit lexical properties (e.g. lexical left-hand stress, such as *bláckbòard*). Answering this question, Liberman and Sproat (1992), Spencer (2003), and Giegerich (2004, 2005), among others, propose the lexicalization analysis of putative root compounds in English. According to this analysis, these are generated as syntactic phrases but may enter into the lexicon to accidentally acquire lexical properties. Following the lexicalization analysis, we assume that the lexical properties come from lexicalization and not from compounding. The lexicalization analysis means that putative root compounds in English are not compounds in a true sense but lexicalized phrases. This is motivated by the fact that their behaviors show no clear word-phrase boundary. In particular, it is well known that putative N-N compounds can have phrasal right-hand stress in some cases but lexical left-hand stress in others. Attributing this inconsistent stress pattern to the gradual nature of lexicalization, Giegerich (2004: 14) states that "[e]nd-stress [= right-hand stress] in *steel bridge*, variable stress in *orange squash* and fore-stress [= left-hand stress] in *orange juice* are probably due to different degrees or diachronic stages of lexicalization" (in the Appendix we explore the lexicalization analysis extensively).

Compounding and lexicalization are different in crucial ways, even though their outputs possess lexical properties. Competition-theoretically, their crucial difference lies in whether they involve structural realization or not. Since compounding is a morphological option for structural realization, it is available in morphology-preferring but not in syntax-preferring languages. On the other hand, lexicalization is not responsible for structural realization but rather operates on realization forms. Since this process is irrelevant to structural realization, it can even be used in syntax-preferring languages like English.

2.4.2. Structural Analysis of Synthetic Compounds

The view that compounding is an option for morphological realization also has implications for the structural analysis of synthetic compounds. There has been substantial debate over their internal structures. For example, *truck driver* has two possible analyses:

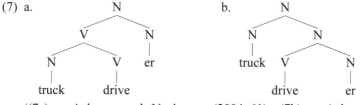

((7a) = Ackema and Neeleman (2004: 61); (7b) = Ackema and Neeleman (2004: 64))

Ackema and Neeleman (2004) point out that Competition Theory necessarily adopts the structural analysis given in (7a) and rules out that given in (7b). This is because *truck driver* does not compete with its syntactic counterpart *driver of truck* in the absence of structural identity (see Section 2.3.1), only if *truck driver* has the structure given in (7a). Ackema and Neeleman (2004: 61) analyze the nominal phrase *driver of trucks* as follows:[4]

---

[4] In (8), 'F' stands for 'functional head.' Ackema and Neeleman regard *of trucks* as an extended projection of *truck*, based on Chomsky's (1981) analysis that *of* is a functional head that is inserted only for the case filter. Therefore, the presence of this preposition does not affect competition.

(8)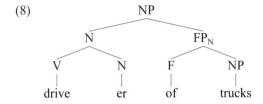

The synthetic compound *truck driver* is the merger of the verbal compound *to truck drive* and the suffix *-er* while the nominal phrase *driver of trucks* is the merger of the two nouns *driver* and *truck*. On the other hand, the analysis given in (7b) leads us to the incorrect prediction that *truck driver* should be in competition with and blocked by *driver of trucks*. According to this analysis, *truck driver* is structurally identical to *driver of trucks* in that both are mergers of two nouns.

The analysis given in (7a) implies that verbs and nouns are directly merged to form verbal compounds within synthetic compounds. As empirical evidence for this analysis, Ackema and Neeleman (2004) point out that synthetic compounds allow nouns and verbs to jointly have idiomatic interpretations in the same way that verbs and arguments have in VPs:

(9) a.   This game usually breaks the ice at parties.
     a'. This game is a great icebreaker at Christmas parties.
                              (Ackema and Neeleman (2004: 56))
     b.   If you **blow the whistle on** someone, or on something secret or illegal, you tell another person, especially a person in authority, what is happening.
     b'. **Whistle-blowing** is the act of telling the authorities or the public that the organization you are working for is doing something immoral or illegal.
                              (COBUILD, s.v. *whistle*, bold in original)

Marantz (1984: 27) observes that idiomatic interpretations require the direct merger of two items. Note that their corresponding nominal phrases lose these idiomatic interpretations (the following '#' denotes absence of the idiomatic reading):

(10) a. #This game is a great breaker of the ice.
     b. #The management were very concerned about the blowing of the

whistle just before the shareholders' meeting.

(Ackema and Neeleman (2004: 56))

According to Ackema and Neeleman (2004), this loss of idiomatic interpretations is due to the fact that nouns do not directly merge with verbs but with derived nouns.

If the analysis given in (7a) is valid, one might wonder why verbal compounds occur when they are embedded within synthetic compounds but not in isolation (e.g. *to truck-drive (Ackema and Neeleman (2004: 49))). In the rubric of 'embedded productivity,' Booij (2010: 47) provides a descriptive generalization for this phenomenon:

(11) The term 'embedded productivity' denotes the phenomenon that a word formation process is normally unproductive, but is productive when it cooccurs with another word formation process.

This phenomenon has called for explanation, having been a mystery in morphology for a long time. Now, a competition-theoretic approach can solve this mystery by capturing 'embedded productivity' as resulting from the failure of competition; there is no syntactic competitor within synthetic compounds because suffixes, e.g. -er and -ing, require morphologically-realized objects as their bases. In this respect, the descriptive generalization given by Booij (2010) above immediately follows from Competition Theory.

We can find another type of 'embedded productivity' in prenominal positions. In the spirit of Competition Theory, Nagano (2013) points out that morphological realization is required for attributive modifiers. She analyzes the italicized compounds in (12) as morphological realizations of attributive modifiers.

(12) a. a *ten-year-old* girl (cf. *ten-years-old* girl)
      b. the *Balkan-weary* troops
      c. *doctor-patient* dialogue
(13) a. a girl who is {ten years old / *ten-year-old}
      b. the troops that are {weary of the Balkans / *Balkan-weary}
      c. dialogue {between a doctor and his or her patient / *between doctor-patient(s) / *that is doctor-patient}

(Nagano (2013: 117))

Chapter 2   The General Architecture of Competition Theory   23

The adjectival compounds *ten-year-old* in (12a) and *Balkan-weary* in (12b) can be paraphrased into the APs *ten years old* in (13a) and *weary of the Balkans* in (13b), respectively. On the other hand, *doctor-patient (dialogue)* in (12c) is an example of what Bauer (2008) calls co-participant compounds. As Olsen (2001: 298–302) points out, they are characteristically interpreted as arguments of relational nouns and paraphrased into PPs, e.g. *between a doctor and his or her patient* in (13c). Notice the ungrammaticality of their predicative usage in (13). They occur only attributively in complementary distribution with their phrasal counterparts. Observing these facts, Nagano (2013) hypothesizes that APs and PPs formally alternate with compounds to function as attributive modifiers.[5] To put it differently, these compound forms are required in the embedded environment, which is successfully captured within the framework of Competition Theory.

2.5.   Main Claim: Clustering Effects of a Single Macroparameter

Within the framework outlined, our inquiry in the following chapters shows that the contrasts listed in Table 2 all result from a single macroparameter determining whether syntactic or morphological realization is default in a given language; they are all reducible to the distinction between syntax-preferring and morphology-preferring languages ('ò' and 'á' in Table 2 denote the position of secondary and main stress, respectively).

---

[5] Nagano (2013) bases her hypothesis on Baker's (2003a, b) analysis, according to which attributive modification requires the overt or covert agreement between modifiers and modifiees. Nagano attributes the phrase-compound alternation to the fact that attributive modifiers must take non-projecting lexical forms to meet this agreement requirement. According to her analysis, the relation between the phrase-compound alternation and the required agreement is confirmed by coocurring formal changes of internal constituents, e.g. the dropping of a plural ending (*ten years͜ old* vs. *ten-year-old*, *weary of the Balkans͜* vs. *Balkan-weary*).

24 *A Study on Cross-Linguistic Variations in Realization Patterns*

Table 2 Contrasts between English and Japanese: Phrases vs. Compounds

	English (Phrases)	Japanese (Compounds)
Predicate · Argument	to wash cars	sen-sya(-suru)
Nominal Modification	òld fámily	kyuu-ka
Resultative Construction	to pound X flat	tataki-nobasu (lit. to pound-spread)
Aspectual Verb Particle Construction	to drink X up	nomi-hosu (lit. to drink-exhaust)
Directional Verb Particle Construction	to take X back	moti-kaeru (lit. to take-return)
'Time'-*Away* Construction	to drink X away	nomi-akasu (lit. to drink-pass)
Body Part Off Construction	to talk one's head off	syaberi-makuru (lit. to talk-turn.up)
Coordination	husband and wife	huu-hu

Table 2 shows that English and Japanese contrast in selecting either phrases or compounds. Assuming that phrases and compounds are syntactically-realized and morphologically-realized forms, respectively, Competition Theory tells us that they are competing forms for realizing the same morphosyntactic structures. English, a syntax-preferring language, selects phrasal forms to syntactically realize a series of morphosyntactic structures. In contrast, Japanese, a morphology-preferring language, selects compound forms for morphological realization. Thus, under Competition Theory, cross-linguistic variations and phrase-compound distinctions can be accounted for in a parallel fashion.

Tables 3 and 4 provide additional examples of contrasts between English and Japanese.

Chapter 2   The General Architecture of Competition Theory   25

Table 3   Contrasts between English and Japanese: Free Forms vs. Bound Forms

	English **(Free Forms)**	**Japanese** **(Bound Forms)**
One-Sided Information Giving	It is raining, I tell you.	Ame-da yo.
Confirmation to the Hearer	It is raining, you know.	Ame-da ne.
Request for Hearer's Agreement	John left, didn't he?	John-wa dekake-masi-ta ne.
Interrogative	What did Mary buy?	Mary-ga nani-o kai-masi-ta ka.

Table 3 indicates that free forms are exploited in English for encoding speech act while their corresponding options in Japanese are bound morphemes that occur sentence-finally.[6]

Table 4   Contrasts between English and Japanese:
 Simplex Forms vs. Complex Forms

	English **(Simplex Forms)**	**Japanese** **(Complex Forms)**
Double Object Construction	to send	okutte-ageru (lit. to send-give)
Benefactive Double Object Construction	to bake	yaite-ageru (lit. to bake-give)
Unergative Construction	to walk	sanpo-suru (lit. to walk-do)
Adposition	under	sita-ni (lit. under-at)

Table 4 states that the same construction takes a simplex form in English but

---

[6] Table 3 suggests that the English wh-word *what* corresponds to the interrogative morpheme *ka* and not to the wh-word *nani* 'what' in Japanese. For the explanation for this correspondence, see fn. 11 in Chapter 4.

a complex form in Japanese. To summarize, the contrast between English and Japanese involves the distinction between free and bound forms in some cases and that between simplex and complex forms in other cases. The point is that from a competition-theoretic point of view the contrasts in Tables 3 and 4 are parallel to the contrast in Table 2, which involves the phrase-compound distinction, in that these contrasts all result from the macroparametric distinction between English and Japanese. Furthermore, Tables 2–4 state that phrasal, free, and simplex forms fall into the same group because they are all used for syntactic realization or morphological-complexity minimizing; on the other hand, compound, bound, and complex forms constitute a natural class as options for morphological realization or syntactic-complexity minimizing.

Furthermore, under Competition Theory, the selection of non-default options is amenable to a principled explanation by assuming that they are available if there is no morphology-syntax competition for some independent reason. In this sense, default and non-default options are treated in a parallel fashion. For example, since verbal compounds are not allowed to occur independently in English (e.g. *to truck-drive), their embedded occurrence (e.g. [N [V truck drive]er]) has been a mystery and been given an exceptional treatment as an instance of 'embedded productivity' in the literature. In contrast, Competition Theory can attribute this embedded occurrence to the failure of the morphology-syntax competition, which is triggered by the requirement that suffixes, e.g. -er and -ing, must take morphological objects as their bases.

The phenomena reviewed in this section have been familiar and extensively discussed. Note, however, that these phenomena have been separately treated in the literature. Within the framework of Competition Theory, these separately-treated phenomena can be given a unified account as instances reflecting the distinction between syntax-preferring and morphology-preferring languages.

2.6. Theoretical Background: Approach Based on Optimality Theory

Competition Theory is based on generative grammar. Certainly, any kind of generative theory may pursue the ultimate goal of elucidating the nature of Universal Grammar (UG), but different theories adopt different approaches to this ultimate goal. While there are some formal generative approaches to language, Competition Theory adopts an approach based on Optimality Theory (OT). While it was originally proposed as a phonological theory by Prince and Smolensky (1993), OT is a general theory of grammar. Therefore, there have been attempts to apply its basic concepts to morphosyntactic phenomena. Competition Theory is among these attempts.

Competition Theory owes some crucial notions and mechanisms to OT. For example, within the framework of Competition Theory, the notions of competition and blocking play a crucial role in determining the well-formed realization form of a given expression. These notions are directly imported from OT into Competition Theory. To illustrate this point, let us take a brief look at the mechanism of OT grammar, which is a device mapping between inputs and outputs. For a given input, the grammar generates and evaluates an infinite set of output candidates, which consists of alternative structural realizations of the relevant input. In this evaluation, candidates compete for the status of being the optimal, and thereby grammatical, output. The candidate that minimally violates the full set of ranked constraints wins this competition and blocks the occurrence of the other competitors; a candidate that violates a lower-ranked constraint beats one that violates a higher-ranked constraint, all other things being equal.

Another notion incorporated from OT into Competition Theory is that a grammar can allow violations of principles or constrains. Within the framework of Competition Theory, this notion is reflected in the idea that non-default realization patterns are available if there is no morphology-syntax competition for some independent reason. The notion of a grammar with violable principles or constraints is closely related to the definition of UG. OT defines UG as a set of universal constraints on outputs that state (un)marked patterns. This definition means that constraints are violable; and violation of a constraint is not a direct cause of ungrammaticality, nor is absolute satisfaction of all constraints essential to a grammar's outputs. Instead what determines the best output of a grammar is the least costly violation of the constraints. Therefore, even in the optimal output a lower-ranked constraint can be violated to avoid the violation of a higher-ranked one. Note that this definition of UG sharply contrasts with that of traditional generative models. According to the traditional definition, UG is a set of inviolable principles and rule schemata (or parameters). Hence, violation of even a single grammatical principle

28   *A Study on Cross-Linguistic Variations in Realization Patterns*

inexorably means ungrammaticality.

To see how the notions of competition, blocking, and a grammar with violable principles or constraints are involved in the determination of the best output in OT grammar, let us consider the appropriateness of the expletive *es* 'it' in German (the capital adverb given in (14b) denotes that an additional stress falls on the adverb):

(14) a.   Es wurde schön   getanzt.
          it was   beautifully danced
          'Someone danced beautifully.'
     b.   SCHÖN   wurde (*es) getanzt.
          beautifully was   it   danced
          'Beautifully, someone danced.'

                                        (Legendre (2001: 7), with slight modifications)

German requires the expletive *es* 'it' to occupy a subject position in impersonal passives, as shown in (14a). However, if an adverb, e.g. *schön* 'beautifully,' conveys new and noteworthy information, the fronted adverb with an additional stress blocks the occurrence of the expletive, as shown in (14b).

According to Legendre (2001), OT attributes this blocking phenomenon to the input by assuming that it encodes information structure features like [new] and [noteworthy]. Elements focused by virtue of encoding these input features are subject to the alignment constraint ALIGNNOTEWORTHY operating in a particular syntactic domain (see McCarthy and Prince (1993)). ALIGNNOTEWORTHY specifies that the focused element is aligned with the left edge of the clause. In (14), this constraint interacts with the two constraints SUBJECT and FULLINT. SUBJECT, capturing the core ideas of the Extended Projection Principle (see Chomsky (1982)), requires that every clause have the highest A-Specifier (Spec IP) filled with a subject. In the same spirit as the Principle of Full Interpretation (see Chomsky (1986)), FULLINT states that lexical items must contribute to the interpretation of a structure. When *schön* 'beautifully' conveys new and noteworthy information as identified in the input, the output given in (14b) is optimal regardless of the violation of SUBJECT, based on its ranking below ALIGNNOTEWORTHY. The competition can be made formally explicit in Tableau 1. The optimal candidate is identified by '☞.' Constraint ranking is indicated by the left-to-right order with each constraint dominating its right ones. The violation of constraints is

Chapter 2   The General Architecture of Competition Theory   29

marked by '*' and the fatal violation is denoted by '*!.'

Tableau 1

	ALIGNNOTE	SUBJECT	FULLINT
(14a): Es wurde schön getanzt.	*!		*
☞(14b): Schön wurde getanzt.		*	

But when no information structure feature is present in the input, ALIGNNOTEWORTHY is vacuously satisfied: SUBJECT requires that Spec IP be filled with an expletive subject. As a result, the output given in (14a) is optimal, though it induces the violation of FULLINT. The result of this competition is schematized in Tableau 2.

Tableau 2

	ALIGNNOTE	SUBJECT	FULLINT
☞(14a): Es wurde schön getanzt.			*
(14b): Schön wurde getanzt.		*!	

The above discussion suggests that the occurrence of expletive subjects in German is tied to a particular constraint interaction that is determined by a particular input. In this sense, the occurrence is sensitive to a syntactic context. This further suggests that the outcome of competition is directly determined by the input. If one adds or removes a feature of the input, the nature of the competition changes because the input determines which of the constraints are applicable.

Here, let us return to the realization patterns of the comparative construction and predicate-argument relationship. Optimality-theoretically, their surface forms can be analyzed as resulting from interaction among constraints. Suppose that UG has a constraint requiring syntactic realization and a constraint requiring morphological realization. By default, the former constraint is ranked higher than the latter in English. Thus, phrasal comparatives are selected as optimal surface forms of underlying structures like [$_{Deg}$ Degree [Adjective]], where the functional Degree and adjectives are merged (e.g. *more symmetric* vs. **symmetricer*). In a similar way, VPs are selected as optimal surface forms of underlying structures like [$_V$ Verb [Noun]], where verbs take nouns as their complements (e.g. *to drive trucks* vs. **to truck-drive*). However, lexical comparatives become optimal in the case of mono-syllabic or di-syllabic adjectives, because a phonological constraint requiring lexical forms is ranked above a constraint requiring syntactic realization (*bigger* vs. **more big*). Likewise, verbal compounds become optimal when they are embedded within synthetic compounds. This is because selectional restrictions on suffixes like *-er*, according to which their bases must be morphological objects, override a constraint requiring syntactic realization (e.g. [N [V *truck drive*]*er*] vs. **[N [VP *drive truck*]*er*]) (see Ackema and Neeleman (2001: 32)).

Finally, let us consider how OT captures cross-linguistic universals and variations. The null hypothesis in OT is that all constraints are universal and cross-linguistic variations derive from alternative rankings of the same constraints. In this sense, OT is inherently typological. This is illustrated by the fact that expletive subjects are obligatory in English but disallowed in Italian: *It rains (*Rains)* vs. *Piove (*Esso piove)* (Haspelmath (2008: 87)). The availability of expletive subjects in a given language depends on the way that SUBJECT and FULLINT are ranked in that language. Since SUBJECT is ranked above FULLINT in English, the expletive *it* is required to occur at the cost of violating FULLINT, which is schematized in Tableau 3.

Tableau 3

English	SUBJECT	FULLINT
☞It rains.		*
Rains.	*!	

On the other hand, FULLINT is ranked higher than SUBJECT in Italian. This ranking disallows the occurrence of *esso* 'it,' which is schematized in Tableau 4.

Tableau 4

Italian	FULLINT	SUBJECT
☞Piove.		*
Esso piove.	*!	

Importantly, the above difference between English and Italian does not mean that some languages have an expletive subject while others do not. OT tells us that even in Italian the occurrence of an expletive subject is forced by pressure of a higher constraint compatible with the satisfaction of SUBJECT. In fact, McCarthy (2002: 110) points out that Italian requires that the subject appear overtly to satisfy SUBJECT when a subject does not have a topic antecedent; thus, OT can account for both variations cross languages and those within a language in a parallel fashion by alternative rankings of universal constraints.

2.7. Summary

This chapter has outlined the general architecture of Competition Theory. This theory is organized into the model of grammar developed by Ackema and Neeleman (2004), which we call the Representational Modularity Model. The core assumption of Competition Theory is that morphology and syntax compete for the PF realization of morphosyntactic structures and that the winner of the competition is parameterized cross-linguistically for each particular language. The morphology-syntax competition obtains only under two conditions: structural and semantic identity. According to the chosen value of the relevant parameter, languages are grouped into syntax-preferring (e.g. English) and morphology-preferring (e.g. Japanese). A parameterized realization pattern is selected by default. A distinctive feature of Competition Theory is that a non-default realization pattern can be selected independently of a parametric value if certain special factors prevent the morphology-syntax competition. Furthermore, Competition Theory assumes that compounding is an option for morphological realization and cannot be used as a default option in syntax-preferring languages. Consequently, root compounds are impossible in English, as a syntax-preferring language, because they should be in competition with and blocked by syntactic phrases. Based on the analysis in the literature, putative root compounds in English (e.g. *ballot box* and *blackboard*) are identified as lexicalized phrases and not as genuine compounds. Within this framework, a wide range of cross-linguistic variations, which have been separately treated in the literature, can be analyzed as clustering effects of a single macroparameter determining a default realization pattern in a given language. These cross-linguistic variations can be given a unified treatment as resulting from the distinction between syntax-preferring and morphology-preferring languages. Competition Theory adopts an OT-based approach: crucial notions and mechanisms, such as competition, blocking, and a grammar with violable principles or constraints, come from OT.

Chapter 3

Realization Patterns of Nominal Modification in English and Japanese*

3.1. Introduction

Under Competition Theory, the selection of a particular realization pattern by a given language is never arbitrary but is instead parametrically regulated. Ackema and Neeleman (2001, 2004, 2005, 2007, 2010) limit their analysis to the surface realization of a predicate-argument structure in Germanic languages. Therefore, it is worth pursuing the applicability of Competition Theory to another case of asymmetrical head-nonhead structures, i.e. a modifiee-modifier structure. This chapter gives a competition-theoretic analysis of surface realizations of the modifiee-modifier structure in English and Japanese. More specifically, we reveal that Baker's (2003a, b) observation on nominal modification immediately follows from Competition Theory. Our analysis in this chapter confirms its far-reaching validity.

---

* The present chapter is a revised version of Nishimaki (2014b). For many stimulating and rewarding discussions on an earlier version of this chapter, I would like to thank Yukio Hirose, Nobuhiro Kaga, Masaharu Shimada, Naoaki Wada, Masaru Kanetani, and Akiko Nagano. I am indebted to two anonymous reviewers for their thought-provoking comments and suggestions. Also I have greatly benefitted from discussions with the following people: Ryuta Fukui, Suguru Mikami, Shuto Yamamura, Masaki Yasuhara, Tatsuhiro Okubo, Keita Ikarashi, Ryohei Naya, and Masanao Asano.

As an example of modifiee-modifier structures, this chapter takes nominal modification by adjectives, which is illustrated in the following translation pairs:

(1) a. an <u>old family</u>   (intended reading: an ancient family)
    a'. kyuu-ka
         ancient-family
         'an old family'

                                                               (= (2) in Chapter 1)
    b. an <u>old book</u>   (intended reading: a secondhand book)
    b'. huru-hon
         secondhand-book
         'an old book'

                          (Kenkyusha's Dictionary, s.v. *huru-hon* 'old book')

In these translation pairs, adjectives modify nouns. The Japanese counterparts of the adjective *old* and the noun *family* in (1a) are *kyuu-* and *-ka*, respectively, in the intended reading, as shown in (1a') (for the adjectival status of *kyuu-* 'old,' see fn. 8). Additionally, the adjective *old* and the noun *book* in (1b) correspond to *huru-* and *hon*, respectively, in the intended Japanese reading, as shown in (1b').[1] Given these considerations, it is safe to assume that the same modification of nouns by adjectives takes phrasal forms in English and compound forms in Japanese.

The organization of this chapter is as follows. Section 3.2 considers Baker's (2003a, b) cross-linguistic observation on an (un)attested type of nominal modification. Section 3.3 gives a competition-theoretic analysis of contrasting realization patterns of nominal modification between English and Japanese. In this analysis, their contrast is attributable to a macroparametric

---

[1] *Kyuu-* 'old' in (1a') and *huru(-i)* 'old' in (1b') are examples of Sino-Japanese (S-J) and native vocabulary, respectively. One might doubt that the former type of vocabulary reflects the characteristics of Japanese because it was borrowed from Chinese. However, it has been proved in the literature that S-J vocabulary has been fully integrated into the linguistic system of Japanese. For example, Shibatani (1990), Kageyama (1993), and Kobayashi (2004), among others, observe that S-J compounds are as productive as native ones, occupying an important part in the vocabulary of Japanese. Also, Nagano and Shimada (2014) demonstrate that S-J and native morphemes mostly form pairs as two distinct ways of reading *kanji* graphs (*on-yomi* and *kun-yomi*). Thus, it is safely assumed that S-J vocabulary raises no problem for discussing the characteristics of Japanese grammar.

Chapter 3   Realization Patterns of Nominal Modification in English and Japanese   35

distinction, and even a non-parameterized, or marked, realization pattern can be accepted if a grammatical environment requires it. Section 3.4 then observes marked realization patterns of nominal modification in English and Japanese.

3.2.   Baker (2003a, b): Cross-Linguistic Variations in Attested Types of Nominal Modification

Based on his theory of lexical categories, Baker (2003a, b) gives a principled explanation for the (un)attestedness of so-called direct modification in English and Japanese. Direct modification is a certain type of nominal modification by adjectives. In the literature, nominal modification by adjectives has been classified into two types: direct and indirect modifications. Before a detailed discussion of Baker's explanation, let us review some differences between these two types of nominal modification.

3.2.1.   Two Types of Nominal Modification: Direct and Indirect Modification

According to Sproat and Shih (1991), attributive adjectives conform to ordering restrictions in direct modification, as in (2a), whereas they are freely ordered in indirect modification, as in (2b).[2]

(2) a.   {small green Chinese / *green Chinese small} vase

                                               (Sproat and Shih (1991: 565))

     b.   {tiisana sikakui / sikakui tiisana} ie
          small   square / square small   house
          'small square house'

                                               (Sproat and Shih (1991: 582))

In (2a), the size adjective *small* must precede the color adjective *green*, which

---

[2] Under the rubric of adjectival nouns (see Kageyama (1993)), adjectives marked with *-na*, e.g. *tiisa-na* 'small,' may be differentiated from those marked with *-i*, e.g. *sikaku-i* 'square.' However, following Baker (2003b), we assume here that these two types belong to the same category 'adjective.'

36   *A Study on Cross-Linguistic Variations in Realization Patterns*

in turn must precede the nationality adjective *Chinese*; the alternation of this word order results in ungrammaticality. In contrast, in (2b), the order of the size adjective *tiisana* 'small' and the shape adjective *sikakui* 'square' does not affect grammaticality. Observing this contrast, Sproat and Shih (1991) assume that adjectives are available for direct modification in English and for indirect modification in Japanese.[3]

In addition, interpretations differ between the two types of modification:

(3) a. Olga is a beautiful dancer.
    b. Olga is beautiful and Olga is a dancer.
    c. Olga dances beautifully.
                                  (Cinque (2010: 9), with slight modifications)

(4) a. Olga-ga   utukusii   odoriko-da.
       Olga-Nom beautiful dancer-Cop.Pres
    b. Olga-ga   utukusiku-te Olga-ga   odoriko-da.
       Olga-Nom beautiful-and Olga-Nom dancer-Cop.Pres
    c. Olga-ga   utukusiku odor-u.
       Olga-Nom beautifully dance-Pres

Cinque (2010) observes that attributive adjectives may be ambiguous between intersective and non-intersective readings in English. When they are indirect modifiers, they may have intersective readings with predicative paraphrases, as shown in (3b). In contrast, when attributive adjectives are direct modifiers, they allow only non-intersective readings with adverbial paraphrases, as shown in (3c). This ambiguity means that English uses adjectives for both direct and indirect modifications (see Cinque (2010)).[4] In Japanese, however,

---

[3] On the basis of ordering restrictions, Sproat and Shih (1991) and subsequent works propose that there is a universal hierarchy of direct attributive adjectives according to their semantic classes. For example, Scott (2002: 114) proposes the following fine-grained hierarchy:

  (i) DETERMINER > ORDINAL NUMBER > CARDINAL NUMBER > SUBJECTIVE COMMENT > ?EVIDENTIAL > SIZE > LENGTH > HEIGHT > SPEED > ?DEPTH > WIDTH > WEIGHT > TEMPERATURE > ?WETNESS > AGE > SHAPE > COLOR > NATIONALITY / ORIGIN > MATERIAL > COMPOUND ELEMENT > NP

The contrast in (2a) is reducible to the fact that size adjectives, e.g. *small*, are higher than color and nationality ones, e.g. *green* and *Chinese*, in this hierarchy.

[4] Given that *dancer* is a deverbal noun, one might suspect that *beautiful dancer* is ana-

Chapter 3　Realization Patterns of Nominal Modification in English and Japanese　37

attributive adjectives have only intersective readings, as is shown by the fact that (4a) can only be paraphrased as in (4b), but not as in (4c). Based on this fact, it is generally assumed that only indirect modification is possible for adjectives in Japanese (see Baker (2003b)).

3.2.2.　Direct Modification as an Adjectival Property

Baker (2003b) attributes the impossibility of direct modification in Japanese to the clausal nature of Japanese adjectives. Baker (2003a, b) assumes that direct modification results from "the merger of a bare noun with a bare 'adjective' in the absence of any distinctively clausal material (Baker (2003a: 252))." Following Sproat and Shih's (1991) insight, Baker (2003b) assumes that nominal modification by adjectives in Japanese is a type of relative clause structure, in which adjectival inflections (e.g. *sikaku-i* 'square' and *tiisa-na* 'small') are fusions of a predicative head with a tense marker. Baker (2003a: 211) proposes the following adjectival parameter:

(5)　In some languages, A[djectives] must be in the minimal domain of a Pred[icate] (Slave, Ika, Japanese, etc.).

Because of this parametric feature, a predicative head intervenes between adjectives and nouns, preventing direct modification in Japanese. In contrast, direct modification is possible in English due to the lack of an intervening predicate in nominal modification.

In Baker's (2003a) theory of lexical categories, only adjectives can quali-

---

lyzed as [N [V *beautiful dance*]er] and not as [NP [A *beautiful*] [N *dancer*]] in the non-intersective reading illustrated in (3c). According to Siegel (1976) and Roeper and Siegel (1978: 221–224), the interpretational ambiguity of nominals like *beautiful dancer* does not come from their structural ambiguity. Following these authors, we assume that they are uniformly the mergers of adjectives and nouns whether they have intersective or non-intersective readings and we do not go into further details. Note that the ambiguity in question may arise even if heads are simplex nouns. For example, in (ia), the simplex noun *friend* is modified by the adjective *old*, which is ambiguous between intersective and non-intersective readings. Respective readings are illustrated in (ib) and (ic).

(i)　a.　Peter is an old friend.
　　　b.　Peter is old and Peter is a friend. (cf. Peter is an aged friend.)
　　　c.　Peter has been a friend for a long time.

(Yamakido (2005: 64))

fy as direct modifiers; neither nouns nor verbs can be direct modifiers. This is a natural consequence of Baker's definition of three lexical categories, which can be formulated as follows:

(6) a. The lexical category N(oun) bears a referential index.
    b. The lexical category V(erb) has a theta-marked specifier (= subject).
    c. The lexical category A(djective) has neither property.

The point is that A is defined as a defective category in (6). Both N and V have theta-theoretic properties. N has a referential index as theta-marked elements and V is a theta-role assigner.[5] In the configuration of direct modification, N and V would induce theta-criterion violations because their theta-theoretic properties cannot be properly licensed. In contrast, A is characterized as having no such character. This category does not have a referential index; nor is it a theta-role assigner. This syntactic defectiveness enables A to involve direct modification. Furthermore, based on behavioral similarities between APs and PPs, Baker (2003a: 311–324) analyzes P(reposition) as a category-shifting functional head that serves to turn NPs into APs.[6] The next section shows that Competition Theory works well in capturing cross-linguistic variations in direct modification, conforming to Baker's classification of grammatical categories and view of direct modification.

---

[5] Baker (2003a) adopts neo-Larsonian clausal structures, in which both a transitive object and a subject are base-generated in a specifier position and both receive a theta-role from a verb there.

[6] For example, APs and PPs can occur as resultative predicates, unlike VPs and NPs:

(i)   I cut the bread {thin / into slices}.   (Baker (2003a: 313))

On the functional status of P, Baker (2003a: 303–311) discusses considerable differences between P, on one hand, and N, V, and A, on the other hand. For instance, P is a closed class, whereas N, V, and A constitute an open class; and P can be neither an input to nor an output of a word formation rule.

Chapter 3   Realization Patterns of Nominal Modification in English and Japanese   39

3.3.   Competition-Theoretic Analysis of Direct Modification

3.3.1.   Japanese A-N Compounds as Morphologically-Realized Forms of Direct Modification

Bearing in mind the observation made in the literature that direct modification is possible in English but not in Japanese, let us consider (1) again, repeated here as (7).

(7) a.   an old family
    a'.   kyuu-ka
       ancient-family
       'an old family'

    b.   an old book
    b'.   huru-hon
       secondhand-book
       'an old book'

As discussed in Section 3.2.1, nominal modification can involve both direct and indirect modification in English. The nominal phrases *old family* in (7a) and *old book* in (7b), for example, involve direct modification. Their interpretation as direct modification can be seen from their non-intersective readings ('ancient family'/'secondhand book') and lack of predicative paraphrases (#*The family is old.*/#*The book is old.*) in the intended reading.[7] Interestingly, it is possible to translate (7a, b) into Japanese, as shown in (7a', b'). This means that the Japanese counterparts of *old family* and *old book*, *kyuu-ka* and *huru-hon* given in (7a', b'), also have an interpretation as direct modification. In fact, the modifiers (*kyuu-*/*huru-* 'old') and the modifiees (*-ka* 'family'/*hon* 'book') establish a non-intersective, but never a predicative, relationship (#*Sono ie-ga hurui.* 'The family is old.'/#*Sono hon-ga hurui.* 'The book is old.').

Recall that Baker (2003b) as well as Sproat and Shih (1991) assume that Japanese only allows the interpretation of indirect modification. The observation made above on the interpretation of (7a', b') seems to contradict this assumption. These authors are right, on the other hand, in the sense that if we translate (7a, b) into Japanese as in (8a, b), the resulting expressions sound rather awkward:

---

[7] On attributive-only adjectives and their status as direct modifiers, see Sproat and Shih (1991: 574) and Cinque (2010: 29–30).

(8) a. hurui ie   b. hurui hon
        old   family   old   book
        'an old family'   'an old book'

In (8a, b), the nouns *ie* 'family' and *hon* 'book' are modified by the adjective *hurui* 'old,' whereby the modifier and the modifiee constitute a nominal phrase. In contrast to the examples in (7a', b'), those in (8a, b) cannot be interpreted as direct modification.

We would like to claim here that the examples in (7a', b') and those in (8a, b) should be differentiated based on whether they are morphological or phrasal. First, consider the examples in (7a', b'), where the modifier and the modifiee form a compound. Specifically, the modifiers *kyuu-* 'old' in (7a') and *huru-* 'old' in (7b') are bound forms.[8] The former is attached with other bound morphemes, such as *-ka* 'family,' to derive words, whereas the latter combines with free forms, such as *hon* 'book.' In contrast, turning to (8a, b), the modifier *hurui* 'old' is not a bound form but a free form, with the modifier and the modifiee combining into a phrasal structure. We are thus led to conclude that direct modification is attested even in Japanese as long as the modifiee-modifier relationship is represented in a word form. In English, on the other hand, direct modification is represented in a phrasal form.

It seems to be implicitly assumed in the literature, such as Sproat and Shih (1991), Baker (2003a, b), and Cinque (2010), that the interpretation of direct modification is exclusively established in the form of syntactic phrases, or that direct modification is just a syntax-specific notion. However, this is not the case. The truth is that an underlying abstract structure for direct modification is available in any language, including English and Japanese. The term 'direct modification' should be used to refer to the structure in which a bare adjective and noun directly merge.

---

[8] One might point out that the categorial status of S-J morphemes is unclear due to their boundness and that it is then questionable whether S-J compounds, e.g. *kyuu-ka* 'ancient family,' are morphological realizations of the direct merger of adjectives and nouns. The relationship between categorial status and boundness is too far-reaching to investigate here. For the present purpose, assuming with Nagano and Shimada (2014) that S-J and native morphemes mostly form pairs as two distinct ways of reading *kanji* graphs (*on-yomi* and *kun-yomi*), we identify categories of S-J morphemes with those of their paired native ones. According to this analysis, a *kun-yomi* variant of the S-J *kyuu-* 'old' is identified with *hurui* because both are written with the same *kanji* (旧／旧い).

Chapter 3 Realization Patterns of Nominal Modification in English and Japanese   41

Under Competition Theory, the cross-linguistic variations and phrase-word distinctions in direct modification observed above are successfully captured. English and Japanese differ with respect to whether they belong to the group of syntax-preferring or morphology-preferring languages. Their surface forms are selected depending on the value of this macroparameter. Competition Theory thus predicts that direct modification is phonologically realized as a form of a syntactic phrase in English and as a form of a morphological compound in Japanese. Indeed, direct modification is observed in phrasal structures in English, whereas it is observed in compound structures in Japanese, as is clearly shown in (7).

Note that direct and indirect modifications do not compete because of their different underlying structures. If we follow Sproat and Shih (1991), Baker (2003a, b), and Cinque (2010), indirect modification is taken as a relative clause structure and distinguished from direct modification in structure. In this sense, the relationship between direct and indirect modification is parallel to the one between *to color-code* and *to code with colors* or the one between *truck driver* and *driver of trucks* (see Chapter 2, Sections 2.3.1 and 2.4.2). Ackema and Neeleman (2004: 82, fn. 11) point out that a relative clause is never in competition with a morphologically-realized form because morphology has no equivalent to a relative operator, which is essential for the semantic interpretation of a relative clause. Because of the lack of a morphological counterpart, indirect modification is possible in Japanese as well as in English.

We provide some additional data on direct modification in English and Japanese. First, let us confirm that Japanese A-N compounds with the interpretation of direct modification are usually translated into English nominal phrases with the interpretation of direct modification, and vice versa. Such translation pairs abound in dictionaries, as shown in Table 5. This correspondence between English and Japanese also suggests the validity of the analysis developed here (stress-marked examples in Table 5 (ii) are quoted from *Longman Pronunciation Dictionary* (Longman), and non-stress-marked ones from Kenkyusha's Dictionary):

42   *A Study on Cross-Linguistic Variations in Realization Patterns*

Table 5   Japanese A-N Compounds and their English Phrasal Counterparts[9]

(i) Japanese	(ii) English	(i) Japanese	(ii) English
aka-niku	rèd méat	kootoo-saibanzyo	Hìgh Córt
aka-singoo	rèd líght	kuro-mazyutu	blàck mágic
anraku-isu	èasy cháir	nan-koogai	sòft pálate
an-situ	dárkroom	niga-warai	bitter smile
ao-enpitu	blùe-péncil	oo-ozi	grèat-úncle
ao-zyasin	blúeprint	ree-sen	còld wár
atu-gesyoo (lit. thick makeup)	heavy makeup	ryoku-tya	grèen téa
		seki-zyuuzi	Rèd Cróss
dai-kigyoo	bìg busíness	sin-iri	néwcomer
haku-syo	whìte páper	sin-keekoo	nèw wáve
haya-ban	early shift	sin-nen	nèw yéar
hituyoo-aku	nècessary évil	siro-ari	whìte ánt
huru-doogu (lit. old furniture)	sècond-hand fúrniture	siro-hata	whìte flág
		siro-kosyoo	whìte pépper
kanree-zensen	còld frónt	siro-mazyutu	whìte mágic
ko-eego	Òld Énglish	tan-pa	shòrt wáve
kok-kai	Blàck Séa	tyoo-ha	lòng wáve
koku-ban	bláckboard	tyoo-on (lit. long-sound)	màjor kéy
koo-kaku	wide-ángle		
koo-koogai	hàrd pálate	uresi-namida	happy tears

---

[9] Japanese (A-N) compounds consistently exhibit compound accents, which indicate their full integration into a phonological unit (see Kageyama (1993, 2009)).

Chapter 3 Realization Patterns of Nominal Modification in English and Japanese 43

The English nominal phrases given in Table 5 (ii) are exclusively involved in direct modification because they are interpreted only non-intersectively (recall from Chapter 2, Section 2.4.1, that under Competition Theory such A-N combinations as those given in Table 5 (ii) are analyzed as syntactic phrases, or rather as syntactically-realized forms of direct modification; combinations like *bláckboard* happen to undergo lexicalization to take on lexical properties, e.g. left-hand stress).[10] For example, *easy chair* does not mean a chair that is easy (= relaxed) but rather one that makes people feel easy while they are sitting in it. The same interpretation is true of the Japanese counterpart *anraku-isu* (lit. 'easy-chair').[11] Therefore, it may be safely assumed that the Japanese A-N compounds in Table 5 (i) involve direct modification in the same way that the English phrasal counterparts do.

Next, we would like to note that A-N compounding is highly productive in Japanese. Its high degree of productivity is indicated by the fact that A-N compounding freely coins new words with consistent compound accents. We find the following recently-coined A-N compounds in *Balanced Corpus of Contemporary Written Japanese Chunagon* (Chunagon Corpus):

(9) adeyaka-mizugi 'fascinating swimsuit'; donkan-otoko 'insensitive man'; henteko-banasi 'ridiculous story'; kuro-situzi 'black butler'; kyuu-kooseesyoo 'former Ministry of Health'; omosiro-burogu 'interesting blog'; sawayaka-gaaru 'lit. refreshing girl = nice girl'; sintookyoo-tawaa 'New Tokyo Tower'; sookai-doraggu 'refreshing drug'; tondemo-hatugen 'absurd statement'; yuru-kyara 'lit. loose character = mascot character'

The high degree of productivity and consistent accents of new A-N compounds suggest that their derivation is regulated by some core component of grammar. The point is that these newly-coined expressions are usually real-

---

[10] For details, see Appendix. Also see Marchand (1969: 64), Allen (1978: 99, 252), Booij (2002a: 316), Spencer (2003), and Hüning (2010: 197). These authors point out that A-N compounds have no productivity in English. In addition, Jackendoff (1997b, 2002b) points out that A-N phrases have the same function as A-N compounds in English.

[11] One might point out that stems of 'adjectival nouns,' e.g. *anraku(-na)* 'easy,' have their categorial status unspecified. This issue goes beyond the scope of our consideration. They are often translated as adjectives in English, as is shown in Table 5. Therefore, for the present purpose, we assume here that they have adjectival status.

44   A Study on Cross-Linguistic Variations in Realization Patterns

ized as words but not phrases.[12, 13] From the viewpoint of Competition
Theory, they are derived through a usual process of merging to form structures
of direct modification. These structures are realized as compounds in accordance with the parametric value that characterizes Japanese as a morphology-
preferring language.

Our competition-theoretic analysis so far has demonstrated that direct
modification is realized as A-N compounds and not as nominal phrases in
Japanese. We would like to conclude this subsection by examining how possible counterexamples to this analysis can be treated. One might suspect that
Japanese A-N compounds may involve indirect modification because they may
coexist with their phrasal counterparts:

(10)   huru-dokee / hurui tokee 'old clock'; maru-gao / marui kao 'round
        face'; adeyaka(na)-mizugi 'fascinating swimsuit'

However, it is reasonable to suppose that these compounds semantically differ
from their phrasal counterparts, because the former cannot alternate with the
latter:

(11)   A: Dotti-ga   seekakuna-no, atarasii tokee soretomo hurui tokee.
            which-Nom accurate-Q   new   clock or   old   clock
            'Which is accurate, a new or an old clock?'
        B: {*Huru-dokee / Hurui tokee}-da-yo.
            { antique-clock / old   clock}-Cop.Pre-YO
            'It is the old clock.'

Plausibly, this semantic difference entails structural difference. For example,
huru-dokee involves direct modification with the non-intersective reading 'antique clock,' but *hurui tokee* involves indirect modification with the intersec-

---

[12] One might note the possibility that *kuro* 'black' (*kuro-situzi* 'black butler') in (9) is a
nominal stem. It is true that some stems of color and shape adjectives behave like nouns
(e.g. *ao(-i)* 'blue,' *aka(-i)* 'red,' and *maru(-i)* 'round'), but they exhibit behavior specific to
adjectival stems. For example, they can undergo *-sa* suffixation unlike regular nominal
stems (*kuro-sa* 'blackness' vs. **asa-sa* lit. 'morningness' (OK with the reading 'shallow-
ness')). Given this, we tentatively postulate their adjectival status.
[13] *Kyuu-kooseesyoo* 'former Ministry of Health' in (9) is an example of W⁺ compounds
(see Kageyama (1993, 2009)). Despite its phrasal accent, the full-fledged wordhood is corroborated by its conformity with the LIP. For example, the relevant type of compound disallows syntactic insertion (*kyuu-(*kyodaina)kooseesyoo* '(huge) former Ministry of Health').

Chapter 3 Realization Patterns of Nominal Modification in English and Japanese   45

tive reading 'old clock' of a relative clause. Of course, it may be that such interpretational difference does not directly reflect the structural difference of particular pairs (e.g. *maru-gao / marui kao* 'round face' and *adeyaka(na)-mizugi* 'fascinating swimsuit') because interpretation depends on pragmatic factors to some degree. Consequently, it sounds as if compounds and their phrasal counterparts had the same semantics. Nevertheless, proper contexts enable us to clearly notice the interpretational difference between direct and indirect modifications.[14]

On the other hand, it appears that some nominal phrases involve direct modification in Japanese because of their non-intersective readings. For example, *hurui yuuzin* 'old friend' may be marginally acceptable with the non-intersective reading of *kyuu-yuu* 'long-standing friend.' However, Watanabe (2012: 511, fn. 7) notes that the use of *hurui* is highly indicative of translation of the intended reading; it should instead be expressed by *hurukukara-no (yuuzin)* 'long-standing (friend).' We agree with Hoshi (2002) that *hurui yuuzin* 'old friend' and the like have intersective readings of relative clauses. Hoshi (2002) points out that the seemingly non-intersective reading results from the properties of a Japanese relative clause. Recall from Section 3.2.2 that nominal modification by adjectives in Japanese occurs as a relative clause structure. Since Kuno (1973), a Japanese relative clause has been assumed to contain a zero pronominal and to be licensed by establishing an 'aboutness' relationship with the relative head. On this assumption, Hoshi (2002: 11) explains that the marginal acceptability may arise if a particular interpretation of the zero pronominal contained in *hurui yuuzin* 'old friend' is licensed by the 'aboutness' condition (for a detailed explanation, see Hoshi (2002)). Alternatively, seemingly non-intersective nominal phrases may be listed as such, given that their interpretation may depend on the idiosyncrasies of the lexical items involved. This is illustrated in the fact that unlike *hurui yuuzin*

---

[14] In the following context, the A-N compound *huru-dokee* 'antique clock' and the nominal phrase *hrui tokee* 'old clock' may alternate:

(i) A: Hurui tokee-ga   sukinan-desu.
         old   clock-Focus like-Polite.Pre
         'It is an old clock that I like.'
     B: Iidesu-yo-ne, {hurui-tokee / ?huru-dokee}-wa.
         good-YO-NE {old clock / ?antique clock}-Topic
         'I totally agree with you that an {old / ?antique} clock is good.'

46   *A Study on Cross-Linguistic Variations in Realization Patterns*

'old friend,' *hurui ie* 'old family' and *hurui hon* 'old book' are not open to non-intersective reading. Furthermore, the interpretation may vary from individual to individual. For instance, some speakers may accept *akai wain* with the non-intersective reading of *aka-wine* 'red wine'; according to Morita (2011: 99, fn. 12), however, it cannot be interpreted non-intersectively. It is plausible to reduce idiosyncrasies of lexical items or individual variations to the lexicon. The point is that their seemingly non-intersective readings arise from extralinguistic factors such as contexts and not from the underlying structures of direct modification.

3.3.2. Diversity of Nominal Modifications in Germanic Languages

To this point, we have observed that Competition Theory opens a new perspective on the treatment of direct modification. We have argued that while the same underlying structure of direct modification is available in both English and Japanese, this structure is realized syntactically in English and morphologically in Japanese. This may remind many readers of the issues concerning nominal modifications in Germanic languages. Striking differences have been observed among these languages with respect to whether naming is realized as a compound or a phrase. According to Booij (2002a, 2010) and Hüning (2010), among others, naming is to provide a single concept/entity with a specific name and nominal modification by adjectives has a naming function.[15] Thus, the proposed analysis, if it is on the right track, should

---

[15] The notion of 'naming' contrasts with that of 'description.' This contrast has been often associated with the word-phrase distinction. It seems to be implicitly assumed in the literature that naming and description are specific to words and phrases, respectively (see, for example, Kageyama (1993: 8); Olsen (2000: 898–899); Ito and Sugioka (2001: 6); Bauer (2003: 135); Shimamura (2014)). However, Booij (2010: Ch. 7) points out that naming as well as description can be found in phrases, giving the following analysis of Dutch nominal phrases (also see Jackendoff (1997b, 2002b)):

(i) [...] the Dutch noun phrase *vaderlandse geschiedenis* 'national history,' which is the conventional name for a particular form of history, namely that from the perspective of one's native country. This phrase can be opposed to the phrase *geschiedenis van het vaderland* 'history of the native country,' a descriptive phrase that refers to the history of one's native country.   (Booij (2010: 170))

As many readers may notice, this analysis suggests that naming units like *vaderlandse geschiedenis* 'national history' are interpreted non-intersectively because the adjectives in-

Chapter 3　Realization Patterns of Nominal Modification in English and Japanese　47

have some significance to this traditional issue. Based on the concept of Competition Theory, this subsection explores a unified treatment of a contrast in realization patterns of nominal modification among typologically unrelated languages, such as English and Japanese, and the contrast among typologically related ones, such as German and Dutch.

Booij (2002a: 316) observes that "[i]n German we have systematically AN compounds, Dutch varies, but is rather similar to English, and English has systematically phrases [...]" Hüning (2010) makes a similar observation. The correspondence among these three languages is illustrated in the following:

(12) | *German* | *Dutch* | *English* |
| --- | --- | --- |
| Dunkelkammer | donkere kamer | dark room |
| Festplatte | harde schijf | hard disk |
| Kleinkind | klein kind | small child |
| Kleinbus | kleine bus | small bus |
| Rotwein | rode wijn | red wine |
| Roteiche | rode eik | red oak |
| Tiefdruck | lage druk | low pressure |
| Hochspannung | hoogspanning | high tension |
| Hochsaison | hoogseizoen | high season |
| Schnellzug | sneltrein | fast train |

(Booij (2002a: 317))

For German and Dutch, Hüning (2010: 200) notes that the adjective in phrases is inflected but that it loses its inflection in compounds:

(13) | | *Phrases* | *Compounds* | |
| --- | --- | --- | --- |
| *German* : | schneller Zug | Schnellzug | 'fast train' |
| *Dutch* : | snelle trein | sneltrein | 'fast train' |

Interestingly, given the above observations, Booij (2002a) and Hüning (2010) assume that the abstract structure of modifying a noun by an adjective can be realized by two different forms, a compound or a phrase, and that the two forms are in competition with respect to the naming function.

---

volved, e.g. *vaderlandse* 'national,' can have the adverbial paraphrases, e.g. *from the perspective of one's native country*. As such, we assume that naming follows from direct modification.

48   *A Study on Cross-Linguistic Variations in Realization Patterns*

This assumption indicates that the issue discussed in the last subsection is parallel to the long-standing issue concerning contrastive realization patterns of naming among Germanic languages. It is thus reasonable to expect that Competition Theory could potentially provide an explanation for the facts observed by Booij (2002a) and Hüning (2010). The contrastive behaviors that English and Japanese exhibit in nominal modification are fundamentally the same as those of Germanic languages. Competition Theory can give a unified account of these contrasts.

In fact, Hüning (2010: 206) has already provided an explanation in the spirit of Competition Theory. First, note that German and Dutch are identical in that they are syntax-preferring languages (see Chapter 2, Section 2.3.2). Accordingly, both of them should select phrasal forms for naming units. However, this is not the case for German. According to Competition Theory, this means that morphological and syntactic realizations do not compete with each other in the case of German naming units for a particular reason, with only the morphological realization pattern available. The case of German naming units is thus similar to the case of *truck driver* in English; in the latter case, morphological realization of the verb-object combination is forced for reasons of suffixation.

The difference between German and Dutch in their surface forms of naming units lies in the richness of inflectional morphology. In German, inflectional morphology is rich; when adjectives modify nouns, their inflectional forms vary depending on grammatical contexts (e.g. gender / number / case of nouns and the presence / absence of determiners in nominal phrases). In contrast, the schwa *-e* is the only adjectival inflection in Dutch, and there is no adjectival inflection in English. Observing this fact, Hüning (2010: 206) hypothesizes that the tendency to use either phrases or compounds is linked to the richness of inflectional morphology. Based on this hypothesis, Hüning (2010: 207) explains the German preference for A-N compounds over phrases as follows:

(14)   While there would be form variation inside the 'name' when realized as phrase, the compound has the preferred constant form: *Schwarzmarkt* ['black market']. In this view, the need for compounding is more pressing in German because of the adjectival inflection and the resulting form variation.

Chapter 3   Realization Patterns of Nominal Modification in English and Japanese   49

According to this explanation, the form variation resulting from rich inflections makes a German A-N phrase too unstable to be identified as a single naming unit; in German, the compound is a much better candidate for the naming function. In contrast, a Dutch or English A-N phrase stays unchanged in (almost) all contexts because of poor inflections. In Dutch and English, this formal stability makes an A-N phrase readily identifiable as a name; the realization of the concept as a compound is not necessary.

From the competition-theoretic point of view, the explanation given in (14) means that the rich inflectional morphology and resulting form variation prevent competition between phrasal and morphological realizations and force German naming units to be realized as compounds irrespective of syntactic preference. Recall that in the case of *truck driver* in English, the morphological reason of affixation cancels the syntactic option of realization. Likewise, in the case of naming units in German, the rich inflectional morphology cancels the syntactic option of realization. The same mechanism of Competition Theory is at work in both cases. Competition Theory provides a unified account for the determination of surface forms of modification structures cross-linguistically.

3.4. Competition-Theoretic Predictions in Non-competing Circumstances

As is observed in the cases that involve suffixation in English and varying inflectional forms in German, Competition Theory predicts that marked realization patterns may be available when there is no competition for certain independent reasons. This section confirms that this prediction is correct. In Section 3.4.1, we point out another case involving suffixation, in which English allows the morphological realization of direct modification in the absence of competition with its syntactic counterpart. In Section 3.4.2, we confirm that Japanese can allow the syntactic realization in the absence of competition with its morphological counterpart.

3.4.1. Morphologically-Realized Forms in English

In addition to *truck driver*, English has another case of 'embedded pro-

50　*A Study on Cross-Linguistic Variations in Realization Patterns*

ductivity,' in which direct modification must be morphologically realized (see Chapter 2, Section 2.4.2). In this case, the suffix *-ed*, which derives adjectives such as *blue-eyed*, is involved. Following Beard's (1995) terminology, we refer to the relevant adjectives as Possessional adjectives. In general, they are analyzed as in (15), based on the parenthesized standard paraphrase.

(15)　[[blue-eye]-ed] ('having a blue eye / blue eyes')　(Plag (2003: 153))

This analysis means that the suffix *-ed* attaches to the combination of the modifier *blue* and the modifiee *eye*. Because English is a syntax-preferring language, the modifiee-modifier combination should be realized as a phrase. However, in the case of (15), Competition Theory predicts that the combination *blue eye* is realized as a compound. This combination is embedded within the suffix *-ed*, which requires that its base be morphological. For this morphological reason, a syntactic realization cannot be counted as an option of its realization form. Just as surface forms of verbal compounds are required for the suffix *-er*, direct modification must be morphologically realized in Possessional adjectives; the suffixal requirement prevents competition with syntactically-realized forms.

The wordhood of the modifiee-modifier combinations embedded in Possessional adjectives is confirmed by their conformity with the LIP:

(16)　a.　*[white dirty hair]ed　(cf. white dirty hair)
　　　b.　*[short and violent temper]ed　(cf. short and violent temper)
　　　　　　　　　　　　　　　　　　　(Shimamura (2007: 376))

Unlike the parenthesized phrasal forms, the suffixed modifiee-modifier combinations disallow adjectival stacking, as in (16a), and internal coordination, as in (16b). Thus, the option of morphological realization is utilized in deriving Possessional adjectives.

3.4.2.　Syntactically-Realized Forms in Japanese

Turning to Japanese, Competition Theory tells us that direct modification can be syntactically realized if there is no competition with any morphologically-realized counterpart. This situation can be found in direct modification by nouns, as noted by Morita (2011) and Watanabe (2012). According to Watanabe (2012), Japanese lacks adjectives that denote nationality / origin and

Chapter 3   Realization Patterns of Nominal Modification in English and Japanese   51

material, that is, a set of denominal adjectives called relational adjectives (RAdjs), and genitive NPs are used instead as direct modifiers.[16] Their status as direct modifiers is confirmed by ordering restrictions, which are illustrated in (17).

(17) a.   {aoi garasu-no   / ?*garasu-no   aoi} koppu
         blue glass-Linker /   glass-Linker blue glass
         'blue glass glass'

(Morita (2011: 97))

     b.   {tiisana tyuugoku-no / ??tyuugoku-no tiisana} kabin
         small   China-Gen /   China-Gen   small   vase
         'small Chinese vase'

(Watanabe (2012: 507))

     c.   {hokuoo-no   ki-no   / *ki-no   hokuoo-no}
         North.Europe-Gen wood-Gen / wood-Gen North.Europe-Gen
         isu
         chair
         'North European wooden chair'

(Watanabe (2012: 508))

Note that no ordering restriction is imposed on regular genitive NPs (e.g. *John-no aoi koppu* 'John's blue glass'). Further supporting evidence comes from the fact that the relevant type of genitive NPs cannot be used predicatively with their intended readings:

(18) a. ??Kono koppu-ga   garasu(-no)-da.
        this   glass-Nom glass(-Gen)-Cop.Pre
        'This glass is made of glass.'

     b. ??Kono kabin-ga   tyuugoku(-no)-da.
        this   vase-Nom China(-Gen)-Cop.Pre
        'This vase is from China.'

     c. ??Kono isu-ga   {hokuoo   / ki}(-no)-da.
        this   chair-Nom {North.Europe / wood}(-Gen)-Cop.Pre
        'This chair is {from North Europe / made of wood}.'

---

[16] Morita (2011) and Watanabe (2012) assume that the particle *-no* is either a linker or a genitive case marker, as shown in the English glosses in (17). For convenience, we follow Watanabe (2012) in treating *-no* marked nominal modifiers as genitive NPs.

These facts lead us to the conclusion that certain semantic classes of genitive NPs qualify as direct modifiers in Japanese.

As observed, in *kyuu-ka* 'ancient family,' for example, the combination of a direct modifier and its modifiee is realized as a compound in Japanese because it is a morphology-preferring language. When modifiers denote nationality / origin and material, however, the structure of direct modification is represented as a syntactic phrase; this is because the relevant classes of modifiers cannot occur as adjectives in Japanese for unclear reasons and must take the form of genitive NPs.[17] The option of morphological realization, i.e. A-N compounding, is blocked due to the lack of RAdjs, and there is no competition between morphological and syntactic realizations. Competition Theory requires that the option of syntactic realization be selected in (17).

The phrasal status of the relevant direct modification is corroborated by accent patterns and *Rendaku* (the voicing of the initial consonant of a compound). For example, in the direct modification *ki-no tukue* 'wooden desk,' *ki* 'wood' and *tukue* 'desk' are separately accented, and / tukue / cannot be voiced (e.g. */ ki-no zukue /). In contrast, in the compound *gakusyuu-zukue* 'learning desk,' *gakusyuu* 'leaning' and *zukue* 'desk' constitute a single accent unit, and / tukue / is voiced into / zukue / by *Rendaku*.

Finally, note that Japanese modifiers can lack adjectival forms even if they denote semantics other than nationality / origin and material. This is clear from translation pairs found in an English-Japanese dictionary. The following pairs, which are quoted from *Taishukan's Unabridged Genius English-Japanese Dictionary* (Taishukan's Dictionary), illustrate English RAdjs with meanings other than nationality / origin and material along with their Japanese counterparts:

---

[17] Nagano and Shimada (2015) attribute the lack of RAdjs to the fact that Japanese adjectives must always be agglutinated with a predicate (see Section 3.2.2.). This basic property of Japanese adjectives is inconsistent with that of RAdjs, which specifies that they cannot occur with a predicate because of their status as direct modifiers.

Chapter 3   Realization Patterns of Nominal Modification in English and Japanese   53

Table 6   English Relational Adjectives and their Japanese Counterparts

(i) English	(ii) Japanese	(i) English	(ii) Japanese
administrative center	gyoosee-no tyuusin	natural products	tennen-no sanbutu
atmospheric vapors	taikityuu-no zyooki	personal possessions	kozin-no syozihin
a causal conjunction	genin-no setuzokusi	psychological research	sinrigaku-no kenkyuu
critical acclaim	hihyooka-no syoosan	religious liberty	sinkoo-no ziyuu
daily meditation	mainiti-no meesoo	the Romantic tradition	romanha-no keetoo
earthly joys	konoyo-no yorokobi	supervisionary duties	kantoku-no syokumu
the eastern sky	higasi-no sora	technological advance(s)	kagakugizyutu-no sinpo
economic theories	keezaigaku-no riron	a triangular road-sign	sankakkee-no doorohyoosiki
an editorial post	hensyuusya-no posuto	verbal mistakes	kotobazukai-no ayamari
mathematical formulae	suugaku-no koosiki	a volcanic eruption	kazan-no bakuhatu
a national holiday	kuni-no syukusaizitu	a windy day	kyoohuu-no hi
		a yearly event	reenen-no gyoozi

Notice that the RAdjs all correspond to genitive NPs in Japanese.[18, 19]   This

---

[18] From a competition-theoretic point of view, this correspondence implies that RAdjs in English and genitive direct modifiers in Japanese have a common underlying structure despite the categorial difference in surface forms.   In the same spirit, Nagano and Shimada (2015) attribute the different surface forms to two different operations: conflation and incorporation.   For a detailed discussion on this issue, see Chapter 4, Section 4.4.2.

[19] As many readers may notice, the correspondence suggests that when the nonhead is a free form, compounding tends to be avoided.   Chapter 4, Section 4.3, shows that this tendency ultimately follows from Competition Theory: Japanese preference for bound over free forms is reducible to the macroparametric fact that Japanese is a morphology-preferring

54 *A Study on Cross-Linguistic Variations in Realization Patterns*

correspondence indicates that Japanese uses genitive NPs instead of RAdjs more widely than it is usually considered (for a detailed discussion on English RAdjs and their Japanese counterparts, also see Shimamura (2014)). The above genitive NPs, which do not denote nationality/origin and material, show the property of direct modifiers in being subject to ordering restrictions and having no predicative usage:[20]

(19) a. {kireena higasi-no / ?? higasi-no kireena} sora
    beautiful east-Gen / east-Gen beautiful sky
    'beautiful eastern sky'
  b. ?? Kono sora-ga higasi(-no)-da.
    this sky-Nom east(-Gen)-Cop.Pre
    'This sky is in the east.'

These examples also show that syntactic realization can even be forced in Japanese.[21]

---

language.
[20] It seems that the predicative usage is possible in some contexts:

(i) A: Dotti-no sora-ga higasi?
    Which sky-Nom east
  B: Kotti-no sora-wa higasi(-no)-da.
    This sky-Top east(-Gen)-Cop

However, according to Watanabe (2012: 511–512, fn. 8), the interpretation of the predicative usage illustrated in (i) fundamentally differs from that of genitive NPs used as direct modifiers: the former is highly context-dependent with some possible readings, while the latter needs no contextual support for the unambiguous reading. Furthermore, Watanabe points out that the sentence-final *da* in (i) is in fact a focus marker and irrelevant to predication in the same way that it is in so-called eel sentences, which are illustrated in (ii).

(ii) Boku-wa unagi-da.
   I-TOP eel-Cop

             (Watanabe (2012: 511–512, fn. 8))
[21] Seemingly, N-N compounds coexist with phrasal direct modifications with genitive NPs:

(i) a. hokuoo-kagu   a'. hokuoo-no kagu 'North European furniture'
  b. tep-pi   b'. tetu-no tobira 'iron door'
  c. keezai-riron   c'. keezai-no riron 'economic theory'

If this is the case, one might wonder whether they are in a competing relationship. The N-N compounds in (ia-c) and the phrasal direct modifications in (ia'-c') involve nominal modification and have the same underlying structure in that both are mergers of two nouns. Given these points, N-N compounds appear to be morphological competitors with phrasal

Chapter 3   Realization Patterns of Nominal Modification in English and Japanese   55

3.5. Summary

This chapter has focused on the applicability of Competition Theory to nominal modification. Our analysis has revealed that a competition-theoretic approach enables us to take a fresh look at the behaviors of nominal modification in English and Japanese. It has been observed in the literature that direct modification is possible in English, while it is impossible in Japanese. It is pointed out here, however, that direct modification is sometimes even observable in Japanese. Competition Theory solves the dual problems of how the contrast between English and Japanese is explained and when direct modification is observed in Japanese. Competition Theory also explains the contrast between German and Dutch in nominal modification. Interestingly, our analysis has shown that this contrast is reducible to the same mechanism that determines when direct modification is observed in Japanese.

Competition Theory tells us that direct modification is universally available but that the surface realization of this underlying structure shows morphology-syntax variations. An available option in a given language is determined by its macroparametric value, namely, its preference for using morphological or syntactic means for structural realization. For example, direct modification is realized morphologically as a compound form in Japanese and syntactically as a phrasal form in English. This is a reflection of the macroparametric distinction between these two languages: Japanese is a morphology-preferring language, whereas English is a syntax-preferring language. In non-competing circumstances, the remaining option is always available for surface forms.

---

direct modifications with genitive NPs. However, if the present analysis is valid, they should not compete. While we are yet to give the exact reason for this failure of competition, a possible explanation is that the relevant direct modifiers as a whole are adjectives, which follows from Baker's (2003a) theory that only adjectives can qualify as direct modifiers (see Section 3.2.2). For similar views, see Morita (2011, 2013) and Nagano and Shimada (2015). Unlike regular Japanese adjectives, the adjectives with -no have no bound form available for A-N compounding. As a result, the phrasal direct modifications are mergers of adjectives with nouns and do not compete with N-N compounds, mergers of two nouns (for an explanation along this line, see Nishimaki (2014a)).

Chapter 4

Further Applications

4.1. Introduction

This chapter explores further possibilities of Competition Theory by applying the analysis developed in Chapter 3 to other grammatical phenomena in which competition between realization patterns may be involved. Competition Theory postulates a macroparameter that determines whether syntactic or morphological realization is selected by default in a given language. A macroparameter is characterized by its large-scale consequences (see Chapter 1, Section 1.1). Given this characterization, it is predicted that in addition to cross-linguistic variations in nominal modification, there should be other phenomena that can be accounted for as consequences of the relevant macroparameter. To prove the correctness of this prediction, this chapter explores the possibility that various contrasts between English and Japanese can be captured as consequences of the single macroparameter, which can be observed across constructions and categories. Phenomena to be dealt with in this chapter have received separate treatment in the literature, though they have been exhaustively discussed. Our exploration shows that these separately-treated phenomena can be given a unified account as manifestations of the distinction between syntax-preferring and morphology-preferring languages.

The organization of this chapter is as follows. Section 4.2 deals with

57

two additional cases in which English and Japanese contrast as to whether phrasal or compound forms are selected for structural realization. One involves resultative constructions and the other coordinated structures. In the former case, the contrast between English and Japanese manifests itself as the distinction between VPs and V-V compounds. In the latter, it shows up as the distinction between phrasal coordinations and coordinated compounds. In either case, as with direct modification, English and Japanese select phrasal and compound forms, respectively, for structural realization. Focusing on discourse markers, Section 4.3 demonstrates that cross-linguistic variations in realization forms can also involve the distinction between free and bound forms. English uses free forms as discourse markers, e.g. speech act markers, while Japanese uses bound forms. Section 4.4 analyzes cross-linguistic variations in head movement. In the literature, it has been pointed out that there are two types of head movement and cross-linguistic variations in which type is preferably used. We demonstrate that these cross-linguistic variations can be analyzed as resulting from the distinction between syntax-preferring and morphology-preferring languages, and we observe contrasting realization patterns of some constructions involved in head movement.

4.2. Phrasal Realization vs. Compound Realization

4.2.1. VPs vs. V-V Compounds

Roughly speaking, resultative constructions express an accomplishment eventuality by describing resultant sates of verbal objects. Competition Theory predicts that English, a syntax-preferring language, adopts a way of syntactic realization to produce a resultative construction while Japanese, a morphology-preferring language, expresses resultative meanings with a surface form of a compound. This prediction is borne out by the following translation pair:

(1) a. Hanako <u>pounded</u> the metal <u>flat</u>.
    b. Hanako-ga   kinzoku-o (taira-ni) <u>tataki-nobasi-ta</u>.
        Hanako-Nom metal-Acc (flat)   pound-spread-Past
        'Hanako pounded the metal flat.'

                                    (= (7) in Chapter 1)

Chapter 4   Further Applications   59

The type of sentence illustrated in (1a) is often taken as a typical example of resultative constructions. (1a) states that the action denoted by the verb *to pound* causes a change of state of the object *the metal*, and that the resultant state is denoted by the following resultative predicate *flat*. In (1a), the verb and resultative predicate together form a VP with the intervening object NP. (1b) shows that this VP has a V-V compound as its Japanese counterpart. The left-hand verb *tataku* 'to pound' of the V-V compound in (1b) is parallel to the matrix verb *to pound* in (1a) in that both verbs denote an action resulting in a change of state of an object NP. On the other hand, the right-hand verb *nobasu* 'to spread' in (1b) is a causative change-of-state verb, the resultant state of which corresponds to the resultative predicate *flat* in (1a).[1] Given this correspondence, we are justified in assuming that right-hand verbs serve as resultative predicates in Japanese V-V compounds.

Kageyama (1996) and Washio (1997) observe that Japanese phrasal resultatives are rather severely restricted in a way that English ones are not. For example, if we translate (1a) into Japanese using a phrasal form, the resultant expression is ungrammatical:

(2) *Hanako-ga   kinzoku-o taira-ni tatai-ta.
    Hanako-Nom metal-Acc flat   pound-Past
    'Hanako pounded the metal flat.'

                    (Kageyama (1996: 209), with slight modifications)

On the other hand, according to Hasegawa (1999), a V-V compound is impossible in English:

(3) *John shoot-killed (shot-kill or shot-killed) Mary.

                                    (Hasegawa (1999: 199, fn. 14))

---

[1] The compound given in (1b) is an example of native compounds (see Chapter 3, fn. 1). It is likely that there are few compounds with resultative meanings when they are composed of S-J morphemes. The following list seems to almost exhaust the relevant examples:

(i) deki-si(-suru) 'lit. to drown-die = to drown'; too-si(-suru) 'lit. to freeze-die = to freeze to death'; boku-satu(-suru) 'lit. to beat-kill = to beat dead'; koo-satu(-suru) 'lit. to strangle-kill = to strangle'; sya-satu(-suru) 'lit. to shoot-kill = to shoot dead'; si-satu(-suru) 'lit. to stab-kill = to stab dead'

We have no explanation for the reason why compounds with resultative meanings are hardly based on S-J morphemes. We leave this issue open and limit ourselves to the consideration of native compounds.

Nevertheless, one might wonder whether A-V compounds are available in English, where adjectives serve as resultative predicates. Nagano and Shimada (2010: 83) confirm that this is not the case, as shown in the ungrammaticality of English A-V compounds in the following examples:

(4) a. *Mother white-bleached the shirt.
    b. *to clean-wipe, *to open-push, *to shut-slam

In the following discussion, let us investigate how these observations follow from Competition Theory.

To begin with, we consider Washio's (1997) cross-linguistic observation on the (un)attested type of resultative construction. Washio (1997) points out that resultative constructions come into two types: strong and weak resultatives. Weak resultatives involve change-of-state verbs and resultative predicates function to further specify an already encoded change of state:

(5) Mary dyed the dress pink. (Washio (1997: 10))

The verb *to dye* in (5) clearly implies that the color is changed by dying. The resultative AP *pink* is further specifying the notion of 'color' that is already contained in the verb. On the other hand, strong resultatives involve activity verbs. Their lexical semantics is completely independent of the meaning of resultative predicates, which turn activities into accomplishments:

(6) She wiped the table {clean / dry}. (Washio (1997: 13))

In (6), the state denoted by the resultative APs *clean* and *dry* is regarded as completely independent of the semantics of the verb *to wipe*. The overall resultative interpretation must then be determined compositionally by combining the simple activity 'she wiped the table' and the state 'clean / dry' into an accomplishment, expressing a causative change of state. This semantic difference yields the following syntactic contrast:

(7) a. He painted the car in an hour. (Ono (2007: 14))
    b. *Don pounded the wall in an hour. (Tenny (1994: 13))

Change-of-state verbs, e.g. *to paint* in (7a), can occur with the completive *in*-phrase while activity verbs, e.g. *to pound* in (7b), cannot.

From a cross-linguistic point of view, Washio (1997: 8) observes that "languages are divided into two broad types, viz., those (like English) which

Chapter 4 Further Applications 61

permit strong resultatives and those (like Japanese) which do not, though weak resultatives are potentially possible in both types of languages." The possibility of both strong and weak resultatives in English is corroborated by the examples given in (5) and (6). On the other hand, the following contrast shows that Japanese permits weak but not strong resultatives:

(8) John-wa pankizi-o usu-ku {*tatai-ta / nobasi-ta}.
John-Top dough-Acc thin pound-Past / roll.out-Past
'John {pounded / rolled} the dough thin.'

(Washio (1997: 9))

The verb *tataku* 'to pound' does not imply any change of state, whereas the verb *nobasu* 'to roll out' implies a resultant state such as *usu-ku* 'thin.'

Since Washio (1997) made the above observation, it has been commonly assumed that Japanese has no strong resultative. However, Competition Theory enables us to take a fresh look at resultative constructions. From a competition-theoretic perspective, we would like to claim that Japanese morphologically realizes strong resultatives as compounds because it is a morphology-preferring language. Here, let us return to the translation pair given in (1), repeated here as (9).

(9) a. Hanako pounded the metal flat.
    b. Hanako-ga kinzoku-o (taira-ni) tataki-nobasi-ta.
       Hanako-Nom metal-Acc (flat) pound-spread-Past
       'Hanako pounded the metal flat.'

The resultative construction given in (9a) illustrates strong resultatives because the matrix verb *to pound* is an activity verb (see (7b)). Given that this strong resultative in English can be translated into the Japanese V-V compound given in (9b), it is safe to assume that Japanese has strong resultatives in the form of compounds. In fact, the matrix verb *to pound* in (9a) and the left-hand verb *tataku* 'to pound' in (9b) are parallel in that both are activity verbs and denote the action that results in a change of state of an object NP. In addition, the resultative phrase *flat* in (9a) and the right-hand verb *nobasu* 'to spread' in (9b) have similar functions in that both describe the result of the action encoded by an activity verb. Competition-theoretically, strong resultatives are attested even in Japanese as long as they are represented in the compound forms required by its macroparametric value. In contrast to Japanese,

62 *A Study on Cross-Linguistic Variations in Realization Patterns*

English represents strong resultatives in phrasal forms, because it is a syntax-preferring language. For convenience, we refer to V-V compounds realizing strong resultatives as resultative V-V compounds (RVVCs). The present analysis proves valid if we observe that despite their different appearances Japanese RVVCs pattern with English VPs that realize strong resultatives. In the following discussion, we examine their parallelisms more closely.

We find the most evident parallelism in the linear order of the predicates involved. Predicates denoting causal events precede those denoting resultant events. Note that this is no mere coincidence. Hasegawa (1999: 204) points out that this parallel linear order is a manifestation of a universal cognitive constraint, which Li (1993: 499) calls the Temporal Iconicity Condition. This constraint states that the order of predicates should universally mirror the order of (sub)events involved. According to Kageyama (1996: 227–236), English VPs that realize strong resultatives and Japanese RVVCs respect another cognitive constraint in a parallel fashion. The constraint is the Unique Path Constraint, which is proposed by Goldberg (1995: 82). This constraint specifies that resultative constructions cannot simultaneously describe physical motion and an abstract change of state. The Unique Path Constraint explains the following ungrammaticality:

(10) a. *Sam tickled Chris off her chair silly.   (Goldberg (1995: 82))
     b. *Sam-ga   sara-o   nage-wat-ta.
        Sam-Nom plates-Acc throw-break-Past
        'Sam threw plates (against something) and broke them.'
        (cf. tataki-waru 'lit. to pound-break = to smash')
               (Kageyama (1996: 229), with slight modifications)

The English example given in (10a) describes the physical motion of Chris falling off her chair and an abstract change of state in which she becomes silly. In the RVVC given in (10b), the left-hand verb *nageru* 'to throw' implies physical motion of something from one place to another, whereas the right-hand verb *kowasu* 'to break' is a typical example of a change-of-state verb. Note that activity verbs, e.g. *tataku* 'to pound,' can be compounded with change-of-state verbs because the former imply no physical motion.

Another parallelism is that resultative predicates and their corresponding right-hand verbs determine the telicity of the entire sentence. Compare the following translation pairs:

Chapter 4   Further Applications   63

(11) a.   John hammered the metal {for an hour / *in an hour}.

(Wechsler (2005: 259))

b.   John-ga   sono kinzoku-o {iti-zikan   / *iti-zikan-de}
John-Nom the   metal-Acc an-hour.for/   an-hour-in
tatai-ta.
hammer-Past

(12) a.   John hammered the metal flat {*for an hour / in an hour}.

(Wechsler (2005: 259))

b.   John-ga   sono kinzoku-o {*iti-zikan   / iti-zikan-de}
John-Nom the   metal-Acc   an-hour.for / an-hour-in
tataki-nobasi-ta.
hammer-spread-Past

The sentences given in (11a, b) describe events without definite endpoints. This is confirmed by the compatibility with durative adverbials (i.e. *for an hour* in (11a) and *iti-zikan* 'for an hour' in (11b)). The addition of the resultative predicate *flat* in (12a) and the right-hand verb *nobasu* 'to spread' in (12b) turn these atelic sentences into telic accomplishments. As a result, the sentences given in (12a, b) allow completive adverbials (i.e. *in an hour* in (12a) and *iti-zikan-de* 'in an hour' in (12b)) (on telicity and possible time adverbials, see Dowty (1979) and Tenny (1994)).

Finally, resultative predicates and their corresponding right-hand verbs are parallel in that their presence may sometimes introduce arguments:

(13) a.   Sylvester cried his eyes *(out).

(Levin and Rappaport Hovav (1995: 36–37))

b.   me-o naki-harasu 'to cry one's eyes out'
(cf. *me-o naku 'lit. to cry one's eyes')

(Kageyama (1996: 213))

In (13a), the intransitive verb *to cry* can appear with the object *eyes* only when the resultative predicate *out* takes place. The same is true of a Japanese RVVC. In (13b), the intransitive verb *naku* 'to cry' can be followed by the object *me* 'eye(s)' only when it is compounded with the transitive verb *harasu* 'to swell.'

These parallelisms lead us to the reasonable assumption that English VPs encoding strong resultatives and Japanese RVVCs share an underlying structure in which verbs merge with other predicates to express resultative meanings. Competition-theoretically, they are different realization forms of the same structure. English VPs are syntactically-realized forms of this structure whereas Japanese RVVCs are its morphologically-realized forms. Their surface forms are selected depending on the chosen macroparametric value.[2] As with direct modification, thus, a competition-theoretic approach can give a unified account of the cross-linguistic variations and phrase-word distinctions observed in resultative constrictions.

The present analysis tells us that strong resultatives cannot be realized with VP forms in Japanese because they are in competition with and blocked by RVVCs. Nevertheless, it seems that VPs with *-te* 'and,' e.g. *tatai-te kowasu* 'to strike and break,' encode strong resultatives and coexist with RVVCs, e.g. *tataki-kowasu* 'lit. to strike-break = to strike to pieces,' in Japanese. The phrasal status of verbal clusters with *-te* 'and' is confirmed by the fact that they allow syntactic division (e.g. *tatai-te kanzenni kowasu* 'to strike and completely break').[3] Note here that the VPs under discussion semantically differ from RVVCs. According to Kageyama (1993: 107), in RVVCs, two verbs jointly describe a single event with a direct cause-effect relationship. This is not the case with the VPs with *-te* '*and*,' where two verbs describe two different events and do not necessarily have a direct cause-effect relationship, as illustrated in the following examples:

---

[2] In the literature, it has been observed that resultative predicates can be realized as various categories depending on the details of the morphosyntax of a given language. Therefore, it is not particularly strange that resultative predicates are realized as APs or PPs in English and as verbs in Japanese. For example, Baker (2003a: 228–230) points out that verbal resultative predicates exist only in languages with little or no verbal inflection, which include West African and South East Asian languages (the verbal resultative constructions observed in these languages are known as serial verb constructions). In terms of the distinction between macroparameters and microparameters (see Chapter 1, Section 1.1), we may assume that cross-linguistic variations in realization forms of strong resultatives, phrases or compounds, are macroparametric but those in categories of resultative predicates are microparametric.

[3] The categorial status of the morpheme *-te*, occurring in VPs such as *tataite kowasu*, is a controversial issue. Some researchers assume that it is a coordination marker, others assume that it is a gerund or tense marker. Since this issue is too far-reaching to investigate here, we do not go into details. For the present purpose, we assume here that it is a coordination marker.

(14) Hanako-ga   terebi-o kinoo   nandomo   tatai-te,
     Hanako-Nom TV-Acc yesterday many.times strike-and
     kyoo tootoo kowasi-ta.
     today finally break-Past
     'Hanako stroke the TV many times yesterday and finally broke it
     today.'

The RVVC *tataki-kowasu* 'lit. to strike-break = to strike to pieces' is inappropriate to describe the situation given in (14). Given these considerations, we assume that VPs like *tataite kowasu* 'to strike and break' do not encode strong resultatives. Pragmatically, they may allow an interpretation similar to that of RVVCs but it does not result from the structure of strong resultatives (this situation is parallel to the coexistence of seemingly synonymous A-N compounds and nominal phrases, which was observed in Chapter 3, Section 3.3.1).

We go on to consider realization patterns of weak resultatives. English realizes not only strong but also weak resultatives as VPs. However, against our prediction based on Competition Theory, Japanese selects phrasal realization for weak resultatives, just as English. The phrasal status of verbal clusters encoding weak resultatives in Japanese is seen from their syntactic transparency. For example, they permit partial deletion by gapping:

(15) John-wa   pankizi-o   usu-ku (nobasi),
     John-Top dough-Acc thin   roll.out
     Paul-wa   pizakizi-o   usu-ku nobasi-ta.
     John-Top pizza.dough-Acc thin   roll.out-Past
     'John rolled the dough thin and Paul rolled the pizza dough thin.'

Note also that Japanese weak resultatives have adjectives as resultative predicates. We can analyze this selection of a phrasal option as an example in which morphological realization is canceled for an independent reason, if we take a closer look at underlying structures of resultative constructions and a property of Japanese adjectives. More specifically, we can assume that the phrasal realization results from the interaction between the property of Japanese adjectives and a constraint on head movement.

We first assume that resultative constructions have neo-Larsonian VP-shell structures, where matrix verbs take resultative predicates as their complements, as proposed by Hale and Keyser (1997), Hasegawa (1999), Baker

66   *A Study on Cross-Linguistic Variations in Realization Patterns*

(2003a), and Mateu (2012), among others. In addition, we adopt the analysis of Japanese adjectives by Nishiyama (1999, 2005), according to which the consonant / k / following adjectival stems is an independent morpheme realizing the functional head Pred(icate) (it is also worth recalling from Chapter 3, Section 3.2.2, that Japanese adjectives must always be agglutinated with a predicate).[4] Given these considerations, the Japanese weak resultative in (16a) can be assumed to have the underlying structure illustrated in (16b).

(16) a. John-wa pankizi-o usu-ku nobasi-ta.
         John-Top dough-Acc thin   roll.out-Past
         'John rolled the dough thin.'

                                                              (= (8))

---

[4] This analysis is based on Bowers' (1993) predication theory, which states that there is PredP whenever there is predication, empirically motivated by the following conjugation paradigm:

(i)   'high'   'wide'
     present   taka-i   hiro-i
     past   taka-katta   hiro-katta
     presumptive   taka-karoo   hiro-karoo
     conditional   taka-kereba   hiro-kereba
     gerundive   take-ku-te   hiro-ku-te

                                              (Nishiyama (1999: 190))

The bound morpheme -*k* manifests itself overtly in all of their inflectional forms except the present. According to Nishiyama (1999), the present form is obtained by deleting -*k* from the underlying *taka-k-i*, for instance. Even in the present form, -*k* is realized when it is focused by the particle -*mo* 'even':

(ii) Yama-ga   taka-ku-mo   ar-u
      mountain-Nom high-ku-even be-Pres
      'The mountain is even high.'

                                              (Nishiyama (1999: 185))

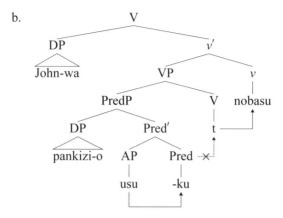

In the configuration given in (16b), the only way to package resultative predicates, e.g. *usu-ku* 'thin,' and matrix verbs, e.g. *nobus* 'to spread,' into a compound form is the successive head movement of adjectival stems into the terminal nodes Pred and V. However, this option is unavailable due to a general constraint on head movement, which Baker (2003a) calls the Proper Head Movement Generalization (PHMG). This constraint is formulated as follows:

(17) A lexical head A cannot move to a functional head B and then to a lexical head C. (Baker (2003a: 53))

The head movement of adjectival stems into V through Pred induces the violation of the PHMG, given that an adjectival stem is lexical, Pred is functional, and V is lexical. In addition, adjectival stems cannot head-move directly into V skipping over Pred, because this head movement induces the violation of the Head Movement Constraint, which is formulated as follows:

(18) An X^0 may only move into the Y^0 which properly governs it.
(Travis (1984: 131))

Consequently, there is no way to realize a weak resultative as a compound form and, thus, the remaining phrasal option is available (see Section 4.4.3 for the underlying structures and derivation of English phrasal resultatives and Japanese RVVCs).

Now that realization patterns of resultative constructions are explained, let us demonstrate that a competition-theoretic approach works well for realization patterns of related constructions. In the literature, it has been pointed

68   *A Study on Cross-Linguistic Variations in Realization Patterns*

out that English resultative constructions have semantically related constructions. Interestingly, English VPs encoding these constructions all correspond
to Japanese V-V compounds in the same way that they do in the case of
strong resultatives. This is illustrated in the following translation pairs:

(19) a.   Elena drank the milk up.   (Jackendoff (2002a: 76))
     b.   Elena-wa   sono miruku-o nomi-hosi-ta.
          Elena-Top the   milk-Acc drink-exhaust-Past
          'Elena drank the milk up.'

(20) a.   Beth took the food back.   (Jackendoff (2002a: 74))
     b.   Beth-wa   sono tabemono-o moti-kaet-ta.
          Beth-Top the   food-Acc   take-return-Past
          'Beth took the food back.'

(21) a.   Fred drank the night away.   (Jackendoff (1997a: 535))
     b.   Fred-wa   sono yoru-o nomi-akasi-ta.
          Fred-Top the   night   drink-pass-Past
          'Fred drank the night away.'

(22) a.   Fred talked his head off, but to no avail.
                                                      (Jackendoff (1997a: 551))
     b.   Fred-wa   syaberi-makut-ta-ga,   muda-dat-ta.
          Fred-Top talk-continue.intensively-Past-but, no.avail-Cop-Past
          'Fred talked his head off, but to no avail.'

According to Jackendoff (2002a), (19a) and (20a) illustrate aspectual and directional verb particle constructions (VPCs), respectively. Although Japanese
has no independent category of verbal particles, we can equate a certain class
of V-V compounds with VPCs (see Kageyama (1993: 126–139, 1996: 248–
250); Kageyama and Yumoto (1997: 75–78)), as shown in (19b) and (20b).
(21a) and (22a) are instances of so-called 'time'-*away* constructions and body
part *off* constructions (BPOCs), respectively (see Jackendoff (1997a)). (21b)
and (22b) show that the Japanese counterparts of these constructions are V-V
compounds whose right-hand verbs are *akasu* 'to pass' and *makuru* 'to continue intensively,' as suggested in Kenkyusha's Dictionary (s.v. *nomi-akasu* 'to
drink the night away' and *syaberi-makuru* 'to talk one's head off').

We can find parallel behaviors in all translation pairs given in (19)–(22).
For example, they behave in a parallel fashion with respect to telicity. It is
well known that aspectual particles, e.g. *up* in (19a), have been semantically

Chapter 4   Further Applications   69

bleached to become pure aspectualizers (see Jackendoff (2002a); Miller (2013)). According to Kageyama and Yumoto (1997: 76), the same is true of their Japanese verbal equivalents, e.g. *hosu* 'to exhaust,' in (19b). The following difference in telicity confirms that they determine the telicity of the entire sentence:

(23) a. He ate our popcorn {for ten minutes / in ten minutes}.

  a′. He ate <u>up</u> our popcorn {*for ten minutes / in ten minutes}.

(Lindner (1983: 171))

  b. Kare-wa watasitati-no poppukoon-o
     he-Top   our-Gen   popcorn-Acc
     {zyup-pun   / zyup-pun-de} tabe-ta.
     ten-minutes.for / ten-minutes-in eat-Past

  b′. Kare-wa watasitati-no poppukoon-o
     he-Top   our-Gen   popcorn-Acc
     {*zyup-pun   / zyup-pun-de} tabe-tukusi-ta.
     ten-minutes.for / ten-minutes-in eat-exhaust-Past

The sentences given in (23a) and (23b) are ambiguous between telic and atelic readings, as shown by the possibility of both durative and completive adverbials (see Tenny (1994: Ch. 1, Sec. 1.2.6) for substantiation of incremental-theme verbs such as *to eat* in (23a) as potentially ambiguous in telicity). However, the aspectual particle *up* in (23a′) and the compounded verb *tukusu* 'to exhaust' in (23b′) force telic readings of these sentences, ruling out durative adverbials.

  Directional particles and their corresponding right-hand verbs also serve as telicity-determiners:

(24) a. The bottle floated (*in an hour).

  a′. The bottle floated <u>away</u> (in an hour).

(Snyder (2012: 290))

  b. Sono tori-wa (*iti-zikan-de) ton-da.
     the   bird-Top an-hour-in   fly-Past
     'The bird flew in an hour.'

  b′. Sono tori-wa (iti-zikan-de) tobi-<u>sat</u>-ta.
     the   bird-Top an-hour-in   fly-away-Past
     'The bird flew away in an hour.'

70   *A Study on Cross-Linguistic Variations in Realization Patterns*

The motion verbs *to float* in (24a) and *tobu* 'to fly' in (24b) are atelic. Thus, they are incompatible with completive adverbials. However, the directional VPC *to float away* in (24a′) and the V-V compound *tobi-saru* 'to fly away' in (24b′) are telic predicates, occurring with completive adverbials.

With respect to 'time'-*away* constructions, Jackendoff (1997a: 537) points out that they rule out inanimate subjects like *light* in (25a) because they require volitionally acting subjects.

(25) a. *The light flashed two hours away.   (Jackendoff (1997a: 537))
     b. *Sono raito-wa   sono yoru-o   tenmetusi-akasi-ta.
         the light-Top the   night-Acc flash-pass-Past
         'The light flashed for the whole night.'
         '(lit.) The light flashed the night away.'

Likewise, corresponding V-V compounds are ruled out if they have inanimate subjects like *raito* 'light' in (25b). In connection with this constraint on subjects, Jackendoff (1997a) further observes that stative verbs like *to sit* in (26a) cannot participate in 'time'-*away* constructions, which require activity verbs.

(26) a. *Celia sat two hours away.   (Jackendoff (1997a: 537))
     b. *Celia-wa   sono yoru-o   sono heya-ni   i-akasi-ta.
         Celia-Top the   night-Acc the   room-in sit-pass-Past
         'Celia sat in the room for the whole night.'
         '(lit.) Celia sat the night away.'

The same is true of Japanese counterparts, as shown in the ungrammaticality of the V-V compound with the stative verb *iru* 'to sit' in (26b).

Finally, according to Jackendoff (1997a), BPOCs must describe atelic events:

(27) a. Sue worked her butt off {for an hour / *in an hour}.
                                       (Jackendoff (1997a: 551))
     b. Sue-wa {iti-zikan   / *iti-zikan-de} tabe-makku-ta
         Sue-Top an-hour.for / an-hour-in   eat-continue.intensively-Past
         'Sue ate his heart off {for an hour / *in an hour}.'

Thus, in (27a), *to work one's butt off* can occur with the durative *for*-phrase but not with the completive *in*-phrase. In the same way, in (27b), the V-V compound *tabe-makuru* 'to eat one's heart off' is atelic, which allows the durative *iti-zikan* 'for an hour' and not the completive *iti-zikan-de* 'in an hour,' though the left-hand *taberu* 'to eat' is itself ambiguous between an atelic and a telic reading (see (23)).

This subsection has discussed resultative constructions, VPCs, 'time'-*away* constructions, and BPOCs. This discussion shows that English and Japanese exhibit the phrase-compound contrasts in realizing a series of constructions. A competition-theoretic approach can provide a unified treatment of these contrasts. It has been well known that complex predicates like resultative constructions have analytic, ie. phrasal, forms in some languages but synthetic, i.e. lexical, ones in others (see Ackerman and LeSourd (1997); Alsina (1997)). However, it remains to be answered where the 'analytic / phrasal-synthetic / lexical' variation comes from. To this question, Competition Theory can answer that the variation in question is a natural reflection of the macroparametric distinction between syntax-preferring and morphology-preferring languages.

4.2.2. Coordinated Structure

Our discussion so far has confirmed the applicability of Competition Theory to asymmetrical headed structures including nominal modification and resultative constructions. This subsection extends our analysis to coordinated structures. The following translation pair exhibits the same phrase-compound contrast that we have observed in asymmetrical structures. Therefore, the contrast points to the applicability of Competition Theory to coordinated structures:

(28) a. The <u>husband</u> and <u>wife</u> cheered each other up.
　　 b. <u>Huu</u>-<u>hu</u>-wa　　　tagai-o　　　hagemasi-ta.
　　　　husband-wife-Top each.other-Acc cheer.up-Past
　　　　'The husband and wife cheered each other up.'

(= (8) in Chapter 1)

In (28a), the presence of the conjunct *and* indicates that the two nouns *husband* and *wife* establish a coordinated relationship, taking a phrasal form. The two nouns *huu-* and *-hu* in (28b) are the Japanese counterparts to *husband* and *wife*, respectively, in (28a). In (28b), these Japanese counterparts make up the dvandva *huu-hu*, which is a compound whose constituents establish a coordinated relationship. Taking a dvandva as a testing ground, this subsection demonstrates that a competition-theoretic approach works well in capturing cross-linguistic variations in coordinated structures.

As the starting point of our discussion, we consider what should be labeled with the term 'dvandva.' There are some types of compounds with coordinative meanings, which may be all called dvandvas in the literature. Following Bauer's (2008) terminology, we refer to compounds with coordinative meanings as coordinative compounds. Bauer (2008) points out that true dvandvas are much fewer than we would normally assume. The term 'dvandva' originates in the Sanskrit grammar. According to Bauer (2008), some types of coordinative compounds are wrongly grouped with dvandvas, because they differ in some crucial points from those identified as dvandvas in Sanskrit. Bauer classifies coordinative compounds into five types:

(29) a. *dvandva*: oya-ko (Japanese) 'lit. parent-child = parent and child'
   b. *appositional*: singer-songwriter
   c. *translative*: London-Edinburgh (express)
   d. *co-participant*: mother-child (relationship)
   e. *hyponym-superordinate*: oak-tree

(Bauer (2008: 4, 7–8, 14))

Semantically, Bauer (2008: 2) defines dvandvas as "understood as being a new unity made up of the whole of the two entities named." The Japanese *oya-ko* 'parent and child' in (29a) means the union of *oya* 'parent' and *ko* 'child.' In this sense, it can be identified as a dvandva. To put it differently, dvandvas consist of two constituents, but they can stand for one concept. For example, Shimada (2013: 90) observes that the Japanese *tyoo-tan* 'lit. long-short = length' can mean the notion of length, but neither to be long nor to be short. Appositional compounds may be most commonly identified as dvandvas in the literature. Excluding them from the set of dvandvas, Bauer (2008: 4) defines these compounds as picking out "the intersection of two sets, and [naming] two aspects of a single individual, not two distinct individuals." For example, *singer-songwriter* in (29b) means the intersection of the set of singers and that of writers and describes two aspects of one person, whereby he is both a singer and a writer. This semantic difference between dvandvas and appositional compounds is better understood from their different Venn diagram representations. According to Bauer (2008: 3–4), the Japanese dvandva *oya-ko* 'parent and child' and the English appositional *singer-songwriter* are represented as Venn diagrams as in Figures 3 and 4.

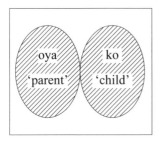

Figure 3   Dvandvas   Figure 4   Appositional Compounds

These diagrams show that appositional compounds denote the intersection of two entities but dvandvas do not.

Let us go on to observe that the other compounds in (29) do not fit the 'two entities but one concept' definition of dvandvas. The translative compound *London-Edinburgh (express)* in (29c) does not denote the combination of the two cities. The same is true of the co-participant compound *mother-child (relationship)* in (29d). This is corroborated by Olsen's (2001: 298–302) observation that these compounds can be paraphrased into postnominal PPs:

(30) a. London-Edinburgh express = express from London to Edinburgh
     b. mother-child relationship = relationship between mothers and children

The hyponym-superordinate *oak-tree* in (29e) means the subset of the tree and not the union of the set of oaks and that of trees.

Bauer (2008) also points out syntactic differences among these five types. In dvandvas, two constitutes function as heads on an equal footing. In contrast, appositional compounds have righthand-headed structures, in which non-heads modify heads. In other words, they belong to the group of attributive compounds. With respect to this contrast, Bauer (2008: 4) states that "[*a*] *jāaváyah* 'sheep and goats' [Sanskrit dvandva] denotes neither a subtype of sheep nor a subtype of goat, while *girl-friend* does denote a subtype of friend." The contrast is more clearly observable if we apply the IS A Condition, which is proposed by Allen (1978), to the relevant compounds. This condition is well known as a criterion for determining heads with the fol-

74   *A Study on Cross-Linguistic Variations in Realization Patterns*

lowing definition:

(31) The IS A Condition
    In the compound $[[....]_X [....]_Y]_{Z'}$
                  Z "IS A" Y   (Allen (1978: 105))

The IS A Condition states that if the compound $[[....]_X [....]_Y]_{Z'}$ can be paraphrased into 'Z is a Y,' Y is a head and Z is the subset of Y. An appositional
compound is sensitive to this condition, as in (32a), but a dvandva is not, as
in (32b).

(32) a. *Singer-songwriter* is a songwriter.
    b. *Oya-ko*-wa   (issyu-no) {#oya / #ko }-da.
       parent-child-Top (a kind of) {#parent / #child}-Cop.Pres
       '(lit.) A parent-child is a {parent / child}.'

This contrast shows that an appositional compound is righthand-headed
whereas a dvandva is not. Similarly, a hyponym-superordinate compound follows the IS A Condition, e.g. *Oak-tree is a tree*. Therefore, this type of coordinative compound can be identified as an attributive compound with a right-
hand head. Let us turn to a syntactic difference between dvandvas and translative / co-participant compounds. Bauer (2008) defines dvandvas as occurring
in isolation. Under this definition, translative compounds (e.g. <u>London-
Edinburgh</u> express (= (29c)) and co-participant compounds (e.g. <u>mother-child</u>
relationship (= (29d)) are not dvandvas, because they can occur only when
they are embedded in prenominal positions, as observed in Chapter 2, Section
2.4.2.

    These considerations lead us to the natural conclusion that only dvandvas
have coordinated structures in a true sense. The other types of coordinative
compounds including appositional compounds, e.g. *singer-songwriter*, constitute a subclass of attributive compounds, though they often have been labeled
as 'dvandvas' in the literature. With this distinction in mind, let us look at
Shimada's (2012, 2013) cross-linguistic observation on dvandvas and appositional compounds.

    Based on Bauer's (2008) classification, as outlined above, Shimada
(2012, 2013) carefully reexamines the typological survey of coordinative compounds by Arcodia et al. (2010). They observe that dvandvas are widely attested in East Asian and South-East Asian languages such as Mandarin

Chinese, Korean, and Japanese, while appositional compounds are restricted to Standard Average European (SAE) languages such as Italian, French, German, and English. Based on this observation, they make the generalization that dvandvas and appositional compounds do not coexist in the same language. In accordance with this generalization, Shimada (2013: 80) summarizes the distribution of dvandvas and appositional compounds as follows:

(33)   Dvandva   Appositional

        SAE   ×   ○

        Asian languages   ○   ×

Shimada examines the validity of this generalization, focusing on English, i.e. an SAE language, and Japanese, i.e. an Asian language. Bauer (2008) observes a few examples of dvandvas in English. However, Shimada demonstrates that they are not dvandvas, and that there is no dvandva in English. On the other hand, Shimada points out that appositional compounds can be found in Japanese. Shimada (2013: 88) gives the following generalization of the (non-)existence of these two types of compound in English and Japanese:

(34)   Dvandva   Appositional

        English   ×   ○

        Japanese   ○   ○

In the following discussion, let us review Shimada's analysis.

Bauer (2008) points out that English has a few examples of dvandvas in certain registers:

(35) a.   Austro-Hungary, Aol-Time-Warner, Hewlett-Packard

                                              (Bauer (2008: 5−6))

     b.   north-west, blue-green   (Bauer (2008: 10, 13))

Shimada (2013: 82) analyzes the expressions illustrated in (35a), which characteristically denote place or business names, as in [*Time-Warner* [*e*]]. In this analysis, they are in fact attributive modifications in which a phonologically null head ([*e*]) is premodified by translative or co-participant compounds. As supporting evidence for his analysis, Shimada (2013: 84) cites the fact that the empty head can be overtly realized with semi-lexical categories (e.g. *Hewlett-Packard Company*). Also, Shimada assumes, with ten Hacken (1994) and Arcodia et al. (2010), among others, that the expressions illustrated in (35b) involve attributive modification. According to his analysis, *north-west* and *blue-green* in (35b) describe a kind of west direction and green color, respectively. Thus, they are righthand headed in conformity with the IS A Condition.

We turn to appositional compounds in Japanese. In the literature, it has been pointed out that these are systematically missing (see Kageyama (2009)). However, Shimada (2013: 87) points out that they are observable even in Japanese:

(36) koomuin-rannaa 'public servant-runner'; kyooin-borantia 'teacher-volunteer'; syuhu-gakusee 'housewife-student'; noomin-sakka 'farmer-writer'; sakka-tomodati 'writer-friend'

Shimada assumes that these compounds are righthand-headed and that *koomuin-rannaa* 'public servant-runner' in (36), for example, means just a kind of runner.

Shimada's (2013) observations naturally follow from Competition Theory, given that English is a syntax-preferring language and Japanese a morphology-preferring language. The observation that dvandvas are attested in Japanese and not in English is logical if we suppose that they are morphologically-realized forms of coordinated structures. Thus, the cross-linguistic variations in dvandvas are successfully reducible to the distinction between syntax-preferring and morphology-preferring languages. The possibility of appositional compounds in Japanese as well as English is also a natural consequence of Competition Theory. If we follow Shimada (2013) in assuming that they are righthand-headed attributive compounds, they can be regarded as morphologically-realized forms of asymmetrical nominal modification in the same way as A-N compounds. To prove the validity of the present analysis, let us make a closer inspection of Japanese dvandvas / appositional compounds and their English phrasal counterparts.

Japanese dvandvas are very productive. Some of their examples, quoted from Shimada (2013: 91-92), are given in the following:

(37) a. N-N: oo-bee 'Europe and America'; ba-syo 'lit. place-place = place'; ka-sen 'lit. river-river = river'; san-ga 'mountain and river'; sa-yuu / hidari-migi 'left and right'; zi-ta 'self and other'

Chapter 4   Further Applications   77

b. V-V: ken-bun / mi-kiki(-suru) 'to look and listen'; omoi-egaku
'to think and picture'; sin-tai 'lit. to proceed-retire =
movement'; soo-zoo(-suru) 'lit. to create-create = to create'; yomi-kaki 'lit. to read-write = reading and writing'

c. A-A: bi-zyaku(-da) 'subtle and weak'; en-kin 'lit. far and near =
distance'; koo-tee 'lit. high and low = height'; sin-sen(-da)
'lit. new-new = new'; zyaku-syoo(-da) 'weak and small'

Observe that these dvandvas are spread across all lexical categories and that
they are consistent in their left-hand accent.[5] In addition to productivity, these
facts suggest that they reflect a core principle of grammar.

One might wonder whether the phrasal expression *otto-to tuma* 'with a
husband, his wife,' for instance, competes with the dvandva *huu-hu* because
they have similar semantics. Relying on Kuno (1973) and Yoda (2010), we
assume that they cannot compete because they have different structures.
According to Yoda (2010), *-to*, which is usually assumed to correspond to the
English coordinator *and*, should be analyzed as a postposition. This analysis
means that *-to* constitutes no coordinated structure because of its postpositional status. We follow Kuno (1973: Ch. 8) in assuming that *-to* corresponds to
the preposition *with* in English. Alternatively, it may be a Japanese counterpart of what Quirk et al. (1985: 761) call quasi-coordinators, e.g. *together
with*, *along with*, and *as well as*. Coordinative expressions with *-to* 'with'
crucially differ from dvandvas in that the former involve nouns but no other
categories:

(38) N-N: otto-to tuma 'with a husband, his wife' (cf. huu-hu 'husband
and wife')

V-V: *omou-to egaku (cf. omoi-egaku 'to think and picture')

A-A: *tikai-to tooi (cf. en-kin 'lit. far and near = distance')

On the other hand, Yoda points out that *sosite*, the Japanese counterpart of the
English *and*, is a true coordinator.[6] Following Yoda's terminology, we refer to

---

[5] Kageyama (1993: 100, 2009: 515) points out that dvandvas and attributive compounds
in Japanese contrast in accent position, while both types have compound accents. Dvandvas
are pronounced with accents on their left-hand constituents. In contrast, attributive compounds put accents on their right-hand constituents.

[6] Yoda observes that *-to* and *sosite* pattern with postpositions and the English *and*, re-

78   *A Study on Cross-Linguistic Variations in Realization Patterns*

coordinative expressions with *-to* as Pseudo Coordinate Structures and to phrasal coordinations with *sosite* (e.g. *otto sosite tuma* 'husband and wife') as Genuine Coordinate Structures. As with Pseudo Coordinate Structures, we assume that Genuine Coordinate Structures do not compete with dvandvas because of their different structures. Observe their semantic difference. Unlike dvandvas, Genuine Coordinate Structures refer to two different entities and not one concept. Plausibly, this semantic difference entails their structural difference.

English syntactically realizes coordinated structures via phrasal coordinations with *and* instead of dvandvas, as shown in the English translations of Japanese dvandvas. Notice that these coordinations are ambiguous between those corresponding to dvandvas and those to Genuine Coordinate Structures. Quirk et al. (1985: 759–762) state that their subject-verb concord disambiguates these two types of phrasal coordination:

(39) a.   Danish bacon and eggs makes a good solid English breakfast.
       b.   Danish bacon and eggs sell very well in London.

(Quirk et al. (1985: 760))

Since in (39a) *bacon and eggs* names a single meal just like a dvandva, the verb *to make* inflects for singular. On the other hand, in (39b), the phrasal coordination corresponding to a Genuine Coordinate Structure has the two different referents *bacon* and *eggs*. Therefore, the verb *to sell* takes a plural inflection. Also, the pronunciation of *and* removes the ambiguity. According

---

spectively. For example, the selectional restriction given in (38) is specific to postpositions and irrelevant to *sosite* and the English *and*:

(i)   a.   [N Ringo] sosite mikan-o   tabetyat-ta.
            apple   and   orange-Acc eat-Past
            'I ate apples and oranges.'
      b.   [A Akai] sosite katai ringo-o   kai-nasai.
            red   and   firm apple-Acc buy-Imp
            'Buy red and firm apples.'
      c.   Kanozyo-wa [V akai ringo-o   {muki/muite/muita}] sosite sasidasi-ta.
            she-Top   red apples-Acc peel   and   give-Past
            'She peeled red apples and gave me them.'

(Yoda (2010: 71))

(ii) a.   [Jane] and [Susan] are well.   (Quirk et al. (1985: 959))
      b.   He specializes in selling [old] and [valuable] books.   (Quirk et al. (1985: 960))
      c.   Yesterday we [bought] and [sold] ten paintings.   (Quirk et al. (1985: 967))

Chapter 4 Further Applications   79

to Taishukan's Dictionary, *and* / ənd / can be reduced into / ən / or / n / (s.v. *and*); coordinated items with the reduced *and* mean a single entity (e.g. *bread and butter* / brédnbˈʌtɚ / 'bread with butter'), while those with the intact *and* refer to two different entities (e.g. *bread and butter* / bréd ənd bˈʌtɚ / 'bread and butter'). The point is that coordinated structures take phrasal forms in English, a syntax-preferring language, whether they correspond to dvandvas or Genuine Coordinate Structures (on coordination in English, also see Kayne (1994: Ch. 6)).[7]

In order to capture the fact that *and* participates in different types of phrasal coordination, we would like to propose that the coordinator has different insertion levels. If a phrasal coordination stands for a single concept, it is not until the final stage of derivation (perhaps Spell-Out) that the insertion of *and* takes place. This type of phrasal coordination is virtually the direct merger of lexical items, where *and* is inserted merely for phrasal realization as parametrically required. Thus, the insertion is done merely to meet the parametric requirement. Because of a direct merger, the relevant type of phrasal coordination can express a single concept in the same way as a dvandva. In this case, *and* surfaces in the reduced form. On the other hand, if a phrasal coordination refers to two different entities, *and* exists at the outset of derivation. In this case, *and* shows up in the intact form. This existence prevents the direct merger at any stage of derivation, which yields different referents (given the revised version of the Representational Modularity Model, which is illustrated in Figure 2 of Chapter 2, we can assume that the intact *and* is inserted from LEXICON into SYNTAX whereas the reduced *and* is inserted at

---

[7] According to Akiko Nagano (personal communication), when we refer to co-authors, we can find the most striking contrast between English and Japanese in selecting either phrasal coordinations or dvandvas. For example, when we talk about a book that Beth Levin and Malka Rappaport Hovav jointly write in 1995, these authors are referred to with the phrasal coordination *and* in English, as illustrated in (i).

  (i) according to Levin and Rappaport (1995)

However, it is impossible to translate this expression into Japanese using -*to* or *sosite*, as shown in (iia, b). If we are to translate it into a natural Japanese expression, we must use a dvandva, as shown in (iic).

  (ii) a. ??Levin-to Rappaport (1995) niyoreba
     b. *Levin sosite Rappaport (1995) niyoreba
     c. Levin・Rappaport (1995) niyoreba

80   *A Study on Cross-Linguistic Variations in Realization Patterns*

PF).

Now, we turn to Shimada's (2013) observation that appositional compounds, which should be identified as attributive compounds, can be found in Japanese. Competition-theoretically, this observation means that Japanese appositional compounds constitute a natural class with attributive N-N compounds like *ha-burasi* 'tooth-brush,' which are morphologically-realized forms of asymmetrical N-N mergers. Therefore, it is predictable that appositional compounds share properties with attributive N-N compounds. This predication is borne out by the fact that appositional compounds are as productive as attributive N-N compounds. We can find the following recently-coined appositional compounds in Chunagon Corpus:

(40)   aidoru-goruhuaa 'idol-golfer'; gakusee-borantia 'student-volunteer'; gakusya-iintyoo 'scholar-chairperson'; gakusya-kanryoo 'scholar-bureaucrat'; gyaru-neesan 'girl-boss'; ikemen-haiyuu 'cool guy-actor'; interi-soobasi 'intellectual-speculator'; kahue-baa 'café-pub'; kahue-gyararii 'café-gallery'; kahue-resutoran 'café-restaurant'; katigumi-zyoyuu 'winner-actress'; kodomo-ninzya 'child-ninja'; mama-tomo 'mother-friend'; mamasan-raidaa 'mother-rider'; obasan-raidaa 'old woman-rider'; ozisan-kyasutaa 'old man-anchorperson'; resutoran-baa 'restaurant-pub'; sakanaya-oyazi 'fishmonger-old man'; sarariiman-ooya 'bussinessman-owner'; sohaa-beddo 'sofa-bed'; syoogaisya-raidaa 'handicapped person-rider'; syuhu-tomo 'housewife-friend'; tarento-bunkazin 'TV personality-intellectual'; tarento-gaka 'TV personality-painter'; tibikko-aidoru 'child-idol'; tibikko-keekan 'child-policeman'

These data suggest that Japanese appositional compounds are more productive than they are normally assumed to be. Also, their conformity to the IS A Condition shows that they are righthand-headed in the same way as attributive N-N compounds:[8]

---

[8] In addition to (41), the following sentence may be acceptable:

(i)   Aidoru-goruhuaa-wa   (issyu-no)   aidoru-da.
      idol-golfer-Top   (a kind of)   idol-Cop.Pres
      'An idol-golfer is an idol.'

We have no clear explanation for this acceptability and leave it open. The acceptability

Chapter 4   Further Applications   81

(41)   Aidoru-goruhuaa-wa   (issyu-no)   goruhwaa-da.
        idol-golfer-Top   (a kind of)   golfer-Cop.Pres
        'An idol-golfer is a golfer.'

Furthermore, the compounds given in (40) all put accents on their right-hand
constituents, which are specific to attributive compounds (see fn. 5).

We go on to consider appositional compounds in English.   Normally, it is
said that they constitute a subclass of root compounds.   Here, recall our assumption that putative root compounds in English are lexicalized phrases and
not compounds in a true sense (see Chapter 2, Section 2.4.1): they are generated as syntactic phrases and enter into the lexicon to acquire lexical properties.   According to this assumption, it follows that appositional compounds
are also lexicalized phrases.   In fact, the lexicalization analysis of appositional
compounds has been proposed in the literature, such as Spencer (2003) and
Giegerich (2004: 11, fn. 10).   Their phrasal nature can be readily found in the
fact that they are consistently even-stressed or righthand-stressed but never
lefthand-stressed (see Marchand (1969: 124); Olsen (2001: 302–303); Plag
(2003: 138); Giegerich (2004: 11)):

(42) a.   king-émperor, qéen móther, prince-cónsort
                                                (Marchand (1969: 124))
      b.   geologist-astrónomer, scholar-áctivist
                                                (Plag (2003: 138))

This consistent phrasal stress points to the possibility that they are true syntactic phrases and not lexicalized at all, as suggested by Marchand (1969: 124).

Finally, we would like to conclude this subsection by pointing out that
seemingly unrelated 'constructions' can receive a unified treatment under
Competition Theory.   In terms of intersectiveness, dvandvas express a non-intersective concept, as seen from Figure 3.   This non-intersectiveness reminds
us of non-intersective readings of A-N compounds.   Recall from Chapter 3
that their non-intersective readings come from the underlying structure in
which a bare adjective and noun directly merge.   Given the same non-intersectiveness, it is reasonable to assume that both dvandvas and A-N compounds

---

may have something to do with the reversibility of appositional compounds.   Olsen (2001)
points out that the order of their constituents is reversible while they have a particular preferred order.

have an underlying structure in which two lexical items directly merge. The difference lies merely in whether coordinated or asymmetrical structures are involved. If so, a competition-theoretic approach can give a unified treatment of dvandvas and A-N compounds as morphologically-realized forms of the direct merger of (two) lexical items. On the other hand, assuming that *sosite* 'and' is some kind of functional head, we may consider its presence to block the direct merger in Genuine Coordinate Structures and that, as a result, they have two different referents. They may be parallel to indirect modifications in that a functional head blocks the direct merger of lexical items in both cases: Chapter 3 observed that the functional head Pred prevents the direct A-N merger and consequently intersective readings occur in indirect modifications. Thus, Competition Theory can nicely capture cross-constructional as well as cross-linguistic universals and variations.

4.3. Free Forms vs. Bound Forms: Realization Patterns of Discourse Markers*

This section observes that discourse markers are realized as free forms in English but as bound forms in Japanese. Our observation reveals that under Competition Theory this 'free-bound' contrast can be accounted for essentially in the same way that the phrase-compound contrast can be.

Let us start our discussion with speech act markers. The contrast in (43) indicates that the combination *I tell you* has a special function.

(43) a. *I tell you that it is so.
    (Ikarashi (2013: 112), quoted from Brown and Levinson (1987: 190))

    b. I tell you, I could fly around this room with my eyes closed!
    (Ikarashi (2013: 113))

---

* The section is a revised version of Nishimaki (2016). For many thought-provoking comments and suggestions on an earlier version of this section, I would like to thank Yukio Hirose, Nobuhiro Kaga, Masaharu Shimada, Naoaki Wada, Masaru Kanetani, and Akiko Nagano.

Chapter 4   Further Applications   83

Regarding this contrast, Ikarashi (2013) observes that in (43a) the speaker and the addressee share the information that something is so while in (43b) the speaker one-sidedly gives to the addressee the information that the speaker could fly around a certain room with his eyes closed. Based on this observation, Ikarashi claims that *I tell you* is used only if the speaker one-sidedly gives information to an addressee who does not know the reported information. This speech act marker roughly corresponds to the particle *yo* in Japanese (see Kuroda (1973); Hirose (1995: 227); Kamio (1994: 71, fn. 6)). Notice their difference in form. *I tell you* is a free form in that it can stand in isolation, while *yo* is a bound morpheme that must occur sentence-finally. Henceforth, we call a particle such as *yo* a sentence-final particle (SFP). Interestingly, according to Ikarashi (2014), *yo* functions as a marker of the speaker's one-sided information giving, just as *I tell you*:

(44) a. Hanako-wa byooki-da yo.   [known only to speaker]
         Hanako-Top ill-Cop.Pre YO
         'Hanako is ill.'

     b. Ii   tenki-da   ne. [known to both speaker and addressee]
         good weather-Cop.Pre NE
         'It's a beautiful day.'

                                              (Ikarashi (2014: 8))

As shown in (44a), *yo* is used if the reported information is only known to the speaker. (44b), where the information is known to both the speaker and the addressee, requires another particle *ne*. Our consideration so far indicates that *I tell you* and *yo* both function to mark the speaker's one-sided information giving. In this sense, these two expressions can be taken to be markers of the same speech act, even though they have different forms.

The same function found in *I tell you* and *yo* leads us to the natural assumption that they have the same underlying structure. According to Rizzi's (1997) Split CP hypothesis, a CP has the following articulated structures:

(45)   ... Force ... (Topic) ... (Focus) ... Fin   IP   (Rizzi (1997: 288))

In terms of this hypothesis, Haegeman (2006) assumes that speech acts are licensed in Force projection, which specifies illocutionary force. Given this assumption, the fact that *I tell you* and *yo* mark the same speech act means that they are licensed in the same Force projection (ForceP). In this respect, they are different realizing forms of the same ForceP. Here, we would like to point out that *I tell you* and *yo* also differ as to whether they occupy either Spec or Head. It has been pointed out that there are cross-linguistic variations as to whether functional projections in the CP domain have their overt realizations at either Spec or Head. With special reference to Force projection, Rizzi (1997: 283) states this point as follows:

(46) Force is expressed sometimes by overt morphological encoding on the head (special C morphology of declaratives, questions, relatives, etc.), sometimes by simply providing the structure to host an operator of the required kind, sometimes by both means (this is the rare case, presumably due to an economy of representation type principle favoring overt expression of a certain substantive specification on the head or on the specifier, but not simultaneously on both: see Cheng (1991), Sportiche (1992)).

In his analysis of the topic-focus system, which is illustrated in (47), Rizzi suggests that English overtly realizes CP Spec.

(47) a. Your book, you should give t to Paul (not to Bill).

(Rizzi (1997: 285))

b.

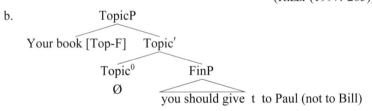

In (47b), the topicalized phrase *your book* is endowed with a Topic feature, when it (or rather the noun *book*) enters into the Numeration; then, this phrase occupies Topic Spec, which results in a Spec-Head configuration. Under this configuration, the Topic feature is checked by the null Topic Head. This being the case, we may safely assume that *I tell you* occupies Force Spec in the same way as the topicalized phrase in (47b). Thus, (48a) can be analyzed as in (48b).

(48) a. I tell you, he is an idiot.   (= (9a) in Chapter 1)

b.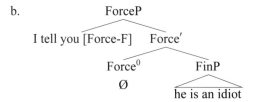

We assume that in (48b) *I tell you* is numerated in one or another way to be endowed with a Force feature, which is checked by the null Force Head under the Spec-Head configuration. On the other hand, Tenny (2006) points out that the SFP *yo* is a head of ForceP (also see Endo (2010, 2014)).[9] For example, according to Tenny, in (49a), *yo* takes scope over the rest of the clause. Thus, (49a) can be analyzed as in (49b), where the Force feature of *yo* is checked by occupying Force Head.

(49) a. Kazuko-wa kinoo Tokyo-e iki-masi-ta yo.
       Kazuko-Top yesterday Tokyo-to go-Polite-Past YO
       'Yesterday Kazuko went to Tokyo (I'm telling you).'

(Tenny (2006: 256))

b.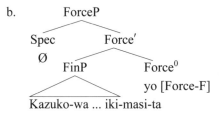

To summarize, English and Japanese contrast in two points regarding realization of speech act. One is that a speech act marker takes a free form in English but a bound form in Japanese; the other is that it occupies Force Spec in English but Force Head in Japanese. A natural question arises of where these contrasts come from. Our observation so far has shown that English and Japanese speech act markers have the same semanticopragmatic function.

---

[9] Haegeman and Hill (2013) propose that speech acts are encoded in an independent projection above ForceP, which they label as Speech Act projection (SAP). Based on this proposal, Murasugi (2011) assumes that the SFP *yo* is hosted in SAP. It does not affect our discussion whether speech acts are encoded in ForceP or in SAP. Thus, for explanatory simplicity, we continue to assume with Haegeman (2006) that speech acts are encoded in ForceP.

Accordingly, it is unlikely that their semanticopragmatic differences yield the observed contrasts. This strongly suggests that they reflect the fundamental distinction between English and Japanese. Below, let us demonstrate that these contrasts come from the distinction between syntax-preferring and morphology-preferring languages.

Note that the distinction between free and bound forms involves the inter-modular distinction between morphology and syntax. By definition, free forms like *I tell you* are atoms visible to syntax, while bound morphemes like *yo* are atoms visible to morphology. Given this, the contrast as to which forms are selected naturally follows from Competition Theory: English, a syntax-preferring language, syntactically realizes speech act using free forms, i.e. syntactic atoms, whereas Japanese, a morphology-preferring language, selects morphological realizations with bound morphemes, i.e. morphological atoms. Thus, from a competition-theoretic perspective, free and bound forms can be viewed as competing forms for structural realization; chosen forms are parametrically determined for each language. We assume that English has no illocutionary morpheme because it can create illocutionary markers, whenever necessary, through the reanalysis of morphosyntactic or morphophonological representations (which is discussed in more detail later). Since *I tell you* is not specialized for speech act, it is available for other purposes. For example, in (50), it is used as a part of a proposition, which is clear from the fact that it is embedded within the subordinate *if*-clause.

(50) If I tell you the car is in the shop, you may conclude you can't ask me for a ride.
(N. Cercone and G. McCalla, *The Knowledge Frontier*, my under-lining)

In other words, *I tell you* is not grammaticalized as a functional category. Therefore, it occupies Force Spec and not Head. In contrast, since *yo* is a functional category listed as an illocutionary maker in the lexicon, it occupies Force Head in the same way as inflections and complementizers.

To pursue the present analysis, let us observe that other types of speech act are consistently marked with free forms in English but with bound SFPs in Japanese. Some examples are given in the following:

(51) a. So he came over to my place, you know.

Chapter 4　Further Applications　　87

b. Sorede　kare-wa　watasi-no　uti-e　　ki-ta　　　no　ne.
so　　　he-Top　my-Gen　home-to　come-Past　NO　NE
'So he came over to my place, you know.'

(Taishukan's Dictionary, s.v. *to know*)

(52) a. John left, didn't he?
b. John-wa　dekake-masi-ta　ne.
John-Top　leave-Polite-Past　NE
'John left, didn't he?'

(Uyeno (1971: 117))

(53) a. What did Mary buy?
b. Mary-ga　nani-o　　kai-masi-ta　　ka.
M.-Nom　what-Acc　buy-Polite-Past　Q
'What did Mary buy?'

(Hasegawa (2005: 49))

Taishukan's Dictionary states that *you know* in (51a) is used when the speaker confirms the propositional content to the addressee. Similarly, according to Kido and Murasugi (2012: 4), the SFP *ne* in (51b) marks the speaker's confirmation to the addressee. The translation pair given in (52) indicates the correspondence between a tag question and the SFP *ne*. They both imply that "the speaker expects to get the addressee's response agreeing with the speaker's supposition as to the given statement (Uyeno (1971: 117))."[10] Furthermore, Hasegawa (2005) points out that English uses wh-words, e.g. *what* in (53a), to encode interrogative force, which Japanese marks with the interrogative SFP *ka* in (53b).[11]

---

[10] One might wonder how tag questions are licensed, because they occur sentence-finally. Adopting Endo's (2009: 111–115) null-operator analysis, we would like to propose that tag questions indirectly establish a Spec-Head configuration with Force Head by way of the movement of a null operator and that their Force features are checked under this indirect Spec-Head configuration. Endo analyzes tag questions as in (i).

(i)　[ForceP John left, [Op didn't he]]?

According to Endo's analysis, tag questions have a null operator, which moves to the Force Spec of the matrix in order to take scope over it.

[11] According to the present analysis, English wh-words and the SFP *ka* bear Force features to encode interrogative force. Note that Japanese wh-words, e.g. *nani* 'what,' do not have this property. Given these considerations, we suppose that English wh-words correspond to the SFP *ka* and not to wh-words in Japanese (see fn. 6 in Chapter 2).

Interestingly, there is another CP domain where English and Japanese contrast in either free forms or bound SFPs. Based on Cinque (1999), Speas and Tenny (2003) and Tenny (2006) propose that a CP hosts Evidential projection (EvidP), which specifies what kind of evidence justifies the utterance. In English, sequences of subjects plus perception verbs may function as evidential markers. For example, according to Anderson (1986), the bracketed *I hear* in (54) ensures that it is from someone else that the speaker has got the information that Mary won the prize. In this sense, *I hear* marks the evidentiality of hearsay.

(54) [I hear] Mary won the prize. ('someone told me')

(Anderson (1986: 274))

Note that in (54) the verb *to hear* carries no sentential stress and that the main predication is the proposition that Mary won the prize. In this respect, evidential usage of *to hear* is distinguished from its normal usage as a perception verb. On the other hand, Aoki (1986) observes that the evidentiality of hearsay is marked with the SFP *tte* in Japanese:[12]

(55) Ame-ga   hutteiru tte.
      rain-Nom falling   TTE
      'They say it is raining.'

(Aoki (1986: 230))

In English, evidential markers may be supplied by syntactic movement. Observing the following contrast, Shizawa (2015a, b) claims that so-called Locative Inversion Constructions are permitted only if the utterance is based on the speaker's direct perception:

---

[12] Interestingly, it has been observed in the literature, such as Mithun (1986) and Aikhenvald (2004), among others, that polysynthetic languages, which constitute the group of morphology-preferring languages, widely use bound morphemes to encode evidentiality, just like Japanese. This is illustrated by the following example from Cherokee, a Native American language spoken at Oklahoma or North Carolina:

(i) u-wonis-eʔi
     he-speak-NON.FIRSTH.PAST
     'He spoke.' (someone told me)

(Aikhenvald (2004: 26))

In Cherokee, the evidentiality of hearsay is marked by the bound morpheme *eʔi* , as shown in (i).

Chapter 4   Further Applications   89

(56) a.   I looked at the door.   Just then, into the room came John.

   b.   *Into the room came John, because the door was left open.

(Shizawa (2015a: 165))

Shizawa's claim suggests that inverted locative phrases like *into the door* in (56a) can be taken as markers of direct evidentiality. Turning to Japanese, Endo (2010: 80) points out that this direct evidentiality is encoded without SFPs (e.g. *Kazi-da Ø.* 'A fire is occurring.') while indirect evidentiality is marked with the SFP *na* (e.g. *Kazi-da na.* 'It seems that a fire is occurring.') for a context in which the speaker merely hears the siren of a fire engine in his room.

Our observation has demonstrated that English realizes discourse markers with various types of free forms, which consistently correspond to bound SFPs in Japanese. Under Competition Theory, a series of correspondences across CP domains can be captured as parallel to the correspondence between *I tell you* and *yo*.

The derivation of discourse markers in English may remain to be solved. Since English does not list discourse markers in the lexicon, they are to be derived somehow. Let us give a brief sketch of the derivation, based on Di Sciullo and Williams' (1987) Coanalysis and Jackendoff's (1997b) Representational Modularity. Di Sciullo and Williams (1987) observe that a single expression can have two independent structures. These authors refer to this dualness of structures as Coanalysis. On the other hand, as mentioned in Chapter 2, Section 2.2, Representational Modularity states that morphosyntactic and morphophonological representations are generated independently from each other. Our assumption is that speech act markers like *I tell you* are derived through the reanalysis of their morphophonological representations generated in one of two independent structures.

Based on Coanalysis and Representational Modularity, we propose that (57a), which contains the speech act marker *I tell you*, is analyzed as in (57b).

(57) a.   I tell you, he is an idiot.   (= (48a))

b.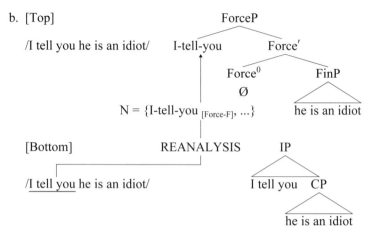

Suppose that the sentence given in (57) has top and bottom structures. In the top structure, *I tell you* is used as a speech act marker and, in the bottom structure, it is a part of a proposition. In both structures, the morphophonological and morphosyntactic representations are generated independently from each other. *I tell you* as a speech act marker exploits its morphophonological representation generated in the bottom structure. This representation is reanalyzed as a single unit. The reanalyzed *I tell you* enters the Numeration of the top structure, where it is endowed with a Force feature. Note that this reanalysis applies only to constituents. According to Nespor and Vogel (1986: Ch. 7), *I tell you*, *I hear*, and *didn't he* constitute intonational phrases, though they are not syntactic constituents. Therefore, their morphophonological, but not morphosyntactic, representations undergo reanalysis. In contrast, sentences with SFPs have mono-structures. For example, (58a) can be assumed to be derived as in (58b).

(58) a. Ame-da yo. 'It is raining, I tell you.' (= (9b) in Chapter 1)

b. /Ame-da yo/

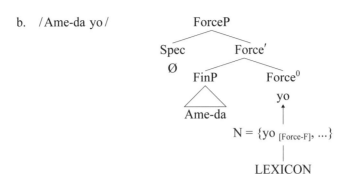

SFPs are numerated from the lexicon, where they are originally listed. As an example, *yo* is endowed with a Force feature in the Numeration.

The present analysis strongly suggests that realization patterns in CP domains differ between syntax-preferring and morphology-preferring languages. Syntax-preferring languages realize functional projections by temporarily-derived free forms at Spec. On the other hand, morphology-preferring languages have realizations with grammaticalized bound morphemes at Head. If the present analysis is on the right track, it has implications for a cartographic approach to clausal structures (see, for example, Rizzi (1997); Cinque (1999, 2006); Cinque and Rizzi (2010)). In the spirit of Chomsky's (2001b) Uniformity Principle (see (3) in Chapter 1), this approach assumes that "all languages share the same functional categories and the same principles of phrase and clause composition, although they may differ in the movements they admit and in the projections they overtly realize (Cinque (2006: 3–4))." On this assumption, recent cartographic works provide a detailed description of cross-linguistic variations in the way that these universal categories are realized. In particular, cartographic works on Japanese have revealed that universal categories hosted in CP domains are realized by various SFPs in this language (e.g. Endo (2009, 2010, 2014); Murasugi (2011); Saito (2012)). However, these works give no explanation for the fundamental question why it must select SFPs as realization forms unlike English. According to the present analysis, this immediately follows from Competition Theory because Japanese is a morphology-preferring language. Thus, under Competition Theory, those cross-linguistic variations that have been separately observed in cartographic works can be given a unified account as instances of the distinction between syntax-preferring and morphology-preferring languages.

Finally, we would like to point out that under the present analysis a language classification proposed in the literature may follow from Competition Theory. The present thesis has demonstrated that languages can be divided into syntax-preferring and morphology-preferring languages within the framework of Competition Theory. In the literature, it has been proposed that languages can also be classified into word-based and stem-based languages. Roughly speaking, this classification depends on the degree to which bound stems are made use of in word formation. Aronoff (1992: 7-8) points out that word-based languages usually define word formation rules on stems that occur as free phonological words, whereas stem-based languages usually define these rules on stems that do not occur as phonologically free words (also see Bloomfield (1933: 225); Ralli (2008: 19-20)). Ralli (2008, 2009), for example, classifies English and Modern Greek into a word-based and a stem-based language, respectively. The present analysis has confirmed that much is made of free and bound forms in syntax-preferring and morphology-preferring languages, respectively. Accordingly, the present analysis suggests that word-based and stem-based languages correspond to syntax-preferring and morphology-preferring languages, respectively. This correspondence points to the possibility that Competition Theory can characterize word-based languages as syntax-preferring languages and stem-based languages as morphology-preferring languages.

4.4. Conflation vs. Incorporation

This section confirms that the distinction between syntax-preferring and morphology-preferring languages may appear as that between operations, with special reference to head movement. In the literature, it has been well documented that there is a typological difference in head movement: the type of head movement that is known as conflation is widely observed in some languages and the type known as incorporation in others (see, for example, Talmy (1985, 1991, 2000); Hale and Keyser (1993, 1997, 1998, 2002, 2005); Baker (1988, 1996, 2003a); Haugen (2008, 2009); Mateu (2012, 2014)). However, there has been no attempt to attribute this typological difference to a fundamental property of the languages in question. This section provides a competition-theoretic analysis of this typological difference. Our analysis reveals that the difference at issue is reducible to the macroparametric distinction between syntax-preferring and morphology-preferring languages and that cross-linguistic variations in constructions involving head movement follow from Competition Theory.

4.4.1. The Distinction between Conflating and Incorporating Languages

To begin with, let us observe the difference between languages that make much of conflation and those that make much of incorporation. For convenience, we refer to the former type of languages as conflating languages and to the latter as incorporating languages. In the literature, English has been treated as a conflating language (e.g. Talmy (1985, 1991, 2000); Hale and Keyser (1993, 1997, 1998, 2002, 2005)). In English, conflation is widely used for verb formation. Let us consider N-to-V conversion. It has been observed that this word formation process is very productive in English (see Clark and Clark (1979)), which is illustrated in the following non-exhaustive list of unergative verbs:

(59) belch, burp, cough, crawl, cry, dance, gallop, gleam, glitter, glow, hop, jump, laugh, leap, limp, nap, run, scream, shout, skip, sleep, sneeze, sob, somersault, sparkle, speak, stagger, sweat, talk, trot, twinkle, walk, yell   (= (10) in Chapter 1))

Hale and Keyser (1993, 1997, 1998, 2002, 2005) propose that N-to-V conflation occurs in N-to-V conversion; for instance, the unergative verb *to laugh* in (60a) derives if the noun *laugh* conflates into a null light verb, as schematized in (60b).

(60) a.　The children laughed.　　　　　　(Hale and Keyser (2002: 14))

　　 b.

(Hale and Keyser (2002: 15), with slight modifications)

A similar N-to-V conflation derives locative, locatum, and subject-experiencer

94   *A Study on Cross-Linguistic Variations in Realization Patterns*

psych verbs, which are illustrated in (61a), (61b), and (61c), respectively.

(61) a. I shelved the books   (Hale and Keyser (2002: 23))
     b. She saddled the horse.   (Hale and Keyser (2002: 19))
     c. I respect Mary.   (Hale and Keyser (2002: 39))

The existence of a wide range of manner verbs also suggests the prominence of conflation in English. The high degree of productivity of these verbs is seen from the following exhaustive list of manner-of-speaking verbs:

(62)   babble, bark, bawl, bellow, bleat, boom, bray, burble, cackle, call, carol, chant, chatter, chirp, cluck, coo, croak, croon, crow, cry, drawl, drone, gabble, gibber, groan, growl, grumble, grunt, hiss, holler, hoot, howl, jabber, lilt, lisp, moan, mumble, murmur, mutter, purr, rage, rasp, roar, rumble, scream, screech, shout, shriek, sing, snap, snarl, snuffle, splutter, squall, squawk, squeak, squeal, stammer, stutter, thunder, tisk, trill, trumpet, twitter, wail, warble, wheeze, whimper, whine, whisper, whistle, whoop, yammer, yap, yell, yelp, yodel   (Levin (1993: 204–205))

According to Harley (2005) and Haugen (2008, 2009), these verbs are derived through manner conflation, in which manner semantics conflates into verbal semantics.

On the other hand, as is well known, polysynthetic languages largely correspond to incorporating languages (see Baker (1988, 1996)). What is characteristic of these languages is a phenomenon known as noun incorporation. The following is an example of noun incorporation from Mohawk, spoken in New York State and neighboring Canada.

(63) a. Owira'a wahrake' ne o'wahru.
         baby   ate   the meat
         'The baby ate some meat.'
     b. Owira'a waha'wahrake'.
         baby   meat-ate

                                        (Baker (2010: 301))

From the NP complement *ne o'wahru* 'the meat' in (63a), the noun *'wahr* 'meat' incorporates into the verb *wahrake'* 'ate' in (63b), which results in the verbal compound *waha'wahrake'* 'meat-ate.' Likewise, Japanese extensively

Chapter 4 Further Applications   95

employs incorporation in word formation (e.g. Shibatani and Kageyama (1988); Kageyama (1993, 2009)). In particular, various kinds of syntactic compounds are derived by noun incorporation, which is illustrated in the following (where '□' denotes accent positions and ':' a slight pause in pronunciation):

(64) a. Yo‾orop‾pa-o ryo‾koo‾-‾tyuu‾
         Europe-Acc   travel-middle
         'while traveling in Europe'

     b. [Yo‾orop‾pa : ryo‾koo‾]-‾tyuu‾
         [Europe : travel]-middle

                              (Shibatani and Kageyama (1988: 460))

(65) a. kinai-ni   kikenbutu-o   motikomi-no   baai-wa
         airplane-in dangerous.goods-Acc bringing.in-Gen case-Top
         'in the case of bringing dangerous goods in an airplane'

     b. kinai-ni   [kikenbutu : motikomi]-no   baai-wa
         airplane-in [dangerous.goods : bringing.in]-Gen case-Top

                              ((65b) = Kageyama (1993: 218))

If noun incorporation applies to the phrase *Yooroppa-o ryokoo(-tyuu)* '(middle of) traveling in Europe' in (64a), it gives rise to the bracketed compound *Yooroppa : ryokoo(-tyuu)* in (64b). In this compound, the noun *Yooroppa* 'Europe' incorporates into the S-J verbal noun *ryokoo* 'travel.' In the same way, the application of noun incorporation to the phrase *kikenbutu-o motikomi* 'bringing dangerous goods in' in (65a) derives the bracketed compound *kikenbutu : motikomi* in (65b). In this compound, the noun *kikenbutu* 'dangerous goods' incorporates into the native verbal noun *motikomi* 'bringing in' (for verbal nouns, see Kageyama (1993)).

   Let us consider the difference between conflation and incorporation in more detail. According to Baker (2003a: 86, 168), the difference is that conflation precedes vocabulary insertion whereas incorporation follows it. This difference leads to the crucial consequence that conflated categories lose their own independent existence in syntax unlike incorporated categories. To put it differently, every element involved in incorporation remains visible after the operation, whereas this is not the case with conflation. Since conflation deprives elements involved of their own independent existence in syntax, conflated X^0 categories exhibit mismatches between semantics and morphophono-

96 _A Study on Cross-Linguistic Variations in Realization Patterns_

logical shapes. In contrast, since every element remains syntactically visible in incorporated X^0 categories, they maintain the exact semantics-morphophonology correspondence. For example, given Perlmutter's (1978: 162) characterization of unergative verbs as predicates describing volitional acts or certain involuntary bodily process, unergatives like _to laugh_ are semantically complex in that they can be decomposed into the two semantic components DO and VOLITIONAL ACT/INVOLUNTARY BODILY PROCESS. These two semantic components are overtly realized in their phrasal paraphrases (e.g. _to laugh_ vs. _to have a laugh_). However, these verbs package the complex semantics into a monomorpheme without overt realization of the verbal semantics DO. The same is true of manner verbs. The following definition of the manner-of-speaking verb _to murmur_ indicates that these simplex verbs have complex semantics:

(66) If you **murmur** something, you <u>say</u> it very <u>quietly</u>, so that not many people can hear what you are saying.

(COBUILD, s.v. _to murmur_, bold in original, my underlining)

According to this definition, _to murmur_ can be semantically decomposed into the verbal component SAY and the manner component QUIET. In contrast, noun incorporation has nouns and verbs overtly realized as separate morphemes in the same way as unincorporated phrases (e.g. _Yooroppa : ryokoo(-tyuu)_ '(middle of) Europe-travel' vs. _Yooroppa-o ryokoo(-tyuu)_ '(middle of) traveling in Europe').

As many readers may notice, our observation so far suggests that conflation and incorporation are used in syntax-preferring and morphology-preferring languages, respectively. In other words, it seems that conflating and incorporating languages correspond to syntax-preferring and morphology-preferring languages, respectively. If so, a natural question is where this correspondence comes from. By giving a principled explanation for the correspondence, the following subsection shows that the distinction between conflating and incorporating languages is reducible to that between syntax-preferring and morphology-preferring languages.

Chapter 4   Further Applications   97

4.4.2.   Competition-Theoretic Analysis of Conflation and Incorporation

Based on the notion of complexity minimizing, the observed correspondence follows from Competition Theory. Recall from Chapter 2, Section 2.3.1, that Competition Theory requires that syntax-preferring and morphology-preferring languages minimize morphological and syntactic complexity, respectively, of realization forms. This being the case, we assume that conflation and incorporation serve to minimize morphological and syntactic complexity, respectively. On this assumption, the prominence of conflation in syntax-preferring languages can be explained as follows. As observed in the last subsection, conflated categories lose their own independent existence in syntax. This means that they have no morphological complexity because they are realized as monomorphemic words, which, by definition, have no internal morphological structure. Therefore, syntax-preferring languages utilize conflation to minimize morphological complexity. Competition-theoretically, conflation is a strategy for creating X^0 categories without morphological complexity.[13] Alternatively, these languages can employ phrasal options, as seen from the fact the conflated simplex verbs like unergatives normally have phrasal paraphrases (e.g. *to laugh* vs. *to have a laugh*). This is because either option will do for minimizing the morphological complexity; therefore, syntax-preferring languages can optionally realize underlying structures in conflated or phrasal forms. Interestingly, from a competition-theoretic perspective, (conflated) simplex words constitute a natural class with phrases in that both are morphological-complexity minimizing forms. Turning to incorporation, every element involved remains visible after the operation. Consequently, incorporated X^0 categories faithfully reflect their morphological derivation from underlying structures to be realized as compounds. In this sense, compounds are

---

[13] Hasegawa (1999: 199, fn. 14) provides an explanation for the ungrammaticality of V-V compounds in English, which is illustrated in (i), stating that "in English a compound with two verbs is in a sense 'too heavy' or 'too complicated' for pure syntactic operations (involving *v* and Tense) to apply."

    (i) *John shoot-killed (shot-kill or shot-killed) Mary.   (= (3))

This heaviness or complicatedness makes perfect sense if we assume that morphological complexity must be minimized as much as possible in English, namely, as a syntax-preferring language.

syntactic-complexity minimizing as well as morphologically-realized forms. Accordingly, morphology-preferring languages use incorporation to minimize the syntactic complexity. Competition Theory can thus characterize conflating languages as syntax-preferring languages and incorporating languages as morphology-preferring languages. In other words, under Competition Theory, we can view conflation as a morphological-complexity minimizing operation and incorporation as a syntactic-complexity minimizing operation. In this sense, conflation and incorporation are competing operations for complexity minimizing.

Let us take a closer look at the derivation of conflated and incorporated X^0 categories. Given the prevailing view of the Minimalist Program, we suppose that head movement is a PF and not a narrow-syntactic operation (see Chomsky (1995, 2001a, 2001b)) whether it involves conflation or incorporation. According to the analysis by Hale and Keyser, the location verb *to shelve* in (67a) can be analyzed as in (67b), where the terminal nodes N, P, and V host the abstract features SHELF, ON, and PUT, respectively.

(67) a. I shelved the books.
　　 b.

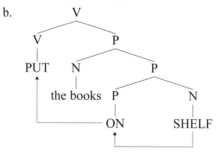

SHELF head-moves into the terminal node P to form the conflated feature bundle {SHELF, ON}, which in turn undergoes head movement into the terminal node V. As a result, the features SHELF, ON, and PUT conflate to be packaged into the single terminal node V. Then, this terminal node undergoes vocabulary insertion and the underlying structure given in (67b) is realized as the monomorphemic verb *to shelve*, as shown in (68).

(68)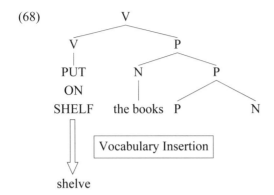

If the underlying structure given in (67b) does not undergo conflation, it has phrasal realization, where the vocabulary items *to put*, *on*, *shelf* are inserted into the terminal nodes V, P, and N, respectively, as shown in (69).

(69)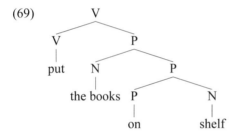

We turn to consider how noun incorporation proceeds. If we follow Shibatani and Kageyama (1988) and Kageyama (1993), the underlying structure of the noun-incorporating compound *Yooroppa : ryokoo(-tyuu)* '(middle of) Europe-travel' in (70a) can be illustrated as in (70b).

(70) a. [Yo|orop|pa : ryo|koo|]-|tyuu|
    [Europe : travel]-middle
    'while traveling in Europe'

(= (64a))

b.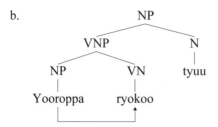

After the vocabulary items *Yooroppa* 'Europe' and *ryokoo* 'travel' are inserted into the terminal nodes N and Verbal Noun (VN), respectively, the noun *Yooroppa* 'Europe' head-moves into VN. This head-movement gives rise to the compound *Yooroppa : ryokoo(-tyuu)* '(middle of) Europe-travel,' as shown in (71).

(71)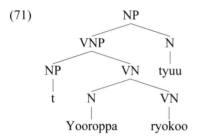

There are some additional facts amenable to a straightforward explanation under the present analysis. Baker (1988) and Hale and Keyser (2002) suggest that noun incorporation is unattested in English. Interestingly, on the other hand, Baker (2003a: 266, fn. 1) suggests that N-to-V conversion is much less productive in polysynthetic languages, e.g. Mohawk and Australian languages, than it is in English. According to Akiko Nagano (personal communication) and Kageyama (1997: 68), the limitedness of N-to-V conversion is true of Japanese. For example, in Japanese counterparts of English converted verbs, nouns and verbs are overtly realized as separate morphemes, as shown in the following examples, which are quoted from Taishukan's Dictionary:

(72) a. *unergative*: sanpo-suru 'lit. to walk-do = to walk' (s.v. *to walk*)
 b. *locative*: hako-ni ireru 'lit. to put in a box = to box' (s.v. *to box*)
 c. *locatum*: kura-o tukeru 'lit. to put a saddle on = to saddle'
   (s.v. *to saddle*)

d. *subject-experiencer*: sonkee-suru 'lit. to respect-do = to respect'

(s.v. *to respect*)

The same holds true for Japanese counterparts of English manner verbs. Masaharu Shimada (personal communication) observes that both manner and verbal components have overt realizations in these counterparts:

(73) *manner-of-speaking*: kogoe-de iu 'lit. to say quietly = to murmur'

(Taishukan's Dictionary, s.v. *to murmur*)

According to the present analysis, these facts are explained as follows. The unattestedness of noun incorporation in English is due to the fact that incorporation is parameterized as a marked option for syntax-preferring languages. By the same reasoning, the limitedness of N-to-V conversion or manner verbs in polysynthetic languages and Japanese is attributable to the markedness of conflation in morphology-preferring languages.

Furthermore, recall from Chapter 3, Section 3.4.2, that Japanese has no RAdj, i.e. denominal adjectives denoting nationality / origin and material, but instead uses genitive NPs (e.g. *ki-no tuke* 'wooden desk') as direct modifiers. Now, this lack of RAdjs in Japanese can be best analyzed as resulting from the markedness of conflation in morphology-preferring languages, if we adopt Nagano and Shimada's (2015) view that the genitive marker *-no* is a category-shifting P in the sense of Baker (2003a). They propose that head movement of nominals denoting nationality / origin and material to the category-shifting P derives so-called RAdjs. They further argue that a process of conflation results in RAdjs (e.g. *wooden*) while a process of incorporation results in genitive NPs (e.g. *ki-no* 'lit. wood-Gen'). Thus, a competition-theoretic approach can nicely capture the (un)attestedness of RAdjs as an instance of the distinction between syntax-preferring and morphology-preferring languages.

Here, we would like to point out that the present analysis may have implications for Baker's (1996) influential Polysynthesis Parameter, which distinguishes polysynthetic languages from other types. Following Ackema and Neeleman (2004: 85–88), the present thesis has assumed that these languages fall into the group of morphology-preferring languages within the framework of Competition Theory (see Chapter 2, Section 2.3.2). This assumption is further supported by the present analysis, according to which the pervasiveness of noun incorporation in polysynthetic languages can be captured as a

102   *A Study on Cross-Linguistic Variations in Realization Patterns*

property specific to morphology-preferring languages. Baker (1996) analyzes this pervasiveness of noun incorporation as an effect of the Polysynthesis Parameter. Given these considerations, the present analysis points to the possibility that under Competition Theory the Polysynthesis Parameter may be attributed to the macroparameter that determines whether a given language is syntax-preferring or morphology-preferring.

4.4.3. Simplex Forms vs. Complex Forms

For further confirmation of the present analysis, this subsection observes that expressions involving head movement take simplex forms in English but complex forms, i.e. compound forms, in Japanese and that this 'simplex-complex' contrast can be analyzed as the conflation-incorporation distinction under Competition Theory. We focus on double object constructions, unergative constructions, resultative constructions, and adpositions.

Let us start with double object constructions (DOCs). Within the framework of Competition Theory, Yasuhara and Nishimaki (2015) propose that Japanese has DOCs in the form of compounds. These authors claim that English DOCs such as (74a) correspond to the Japanese sentences exemplified in (74b) rather than those exemplified in (74c), which are equivalent to English *to*-dative constructions.

(74) a. Taro sent Hanako a letter.
　　　b. Taro-ga　　Hanako-ni　tegami-o　okutte-age-ta.
　　　　　Taro-Nom　Hanako-Dat　letter-Acc　send-give-Past
　　　　　'Taro sent Hanako a letter.'
　　　c. Taro-ga　　Hanako-ni　tegami-o　okut-ta.
　　　　　Taro-Nom　Hanako-Dat　letter-Acc　send-Past
　　　　　'Taro sent a letter to Hanako.'

(Yasuhara and Nishimaki (2015: 584))

For convenience, we refer to Japanese sentences like (74b) as *ageru* constructions because they are characterized by the presence of the verb *ageru* 'to give.' According to Yasuhara and Nishimaki (2015), the correspondence between English DOCs and *ageru* constructions is confirmed by the fact that both types of constructions require indirect objects to be construed as possessors of direct objects. This requirement is the defining property of DOCs, as

Chapter 4 Further Applications 103

pointed out by Marantz (1993) and Pylkkänen (2008), among others. Therefore, English DOCs and *ageru* constructions are incompatible with indirect objects that refer to locations, e.g. *France*. Observe the following ungrammaticality:

(75) a. *John sent France the book.   (Pesetsky (1995:124))
     b. *Taro-ga   France-ni   hon-o   okutte-age-ta.
        Taro-Nom France-Dat book-Acc send-give-Past
                                        (Yasuhara and Nishimaki (2015: 589))

In contrast, the requirement in question is not found in English *to*-dative constructions and Japanese sentences that lack *ageru* 'to give,' as shown in the following:

(76) a. John sent the book to France.   (Pesetsky (1995:124))
     b. Taro-ga   France-ni   hon-o   okut-ta.
        Taro-Nom France-Dat book-Acc send-Past
                  (Yasuhara and Nishimaki (2015: 589), with slight modifications)

These examples indicate that English *to*-datives and their Japanese counterparts can take location DPs as indirect objects.[14]

Notice the difference between DOCs and *ageru* constructions. The former involve simplex verbs (e.g. *to send* in (74a)) but the latter involve compounds (e.g. *okutte-ageru* 'lit. to send-give = to send' in (74b)) (here we leave the categorial status of the morpheme *-te* open (see fn. 3)). Along the line of the analysis developed here, Yasuhara and Nishimaki (2015) attribute this difference to the fact that DOCs derive via conflation but *ageru* constructions via incorporation. Marantz (1993) analyzes DOCs as resulting from the movement of the functional head Appl(icative), which introduces arguments realized as indirect objects (also see Pylkkänen (2008)). Based on this analysis, Yasuhara and Nishimaki (2015) assume that the DOC in (77a) derives as in (77b).

(77) a. Taro sent Hanako a letter.   (= (74a))

---

[14] Prior to Yasuhara and Nishimaki (2015), Kishimoto (2001: 47–48) points out that there is no correspondence between English DOCs and Japanese sentences like (76b) because indirect objects are restricted to possessor DPs in the former but they are not in the latter.

b.

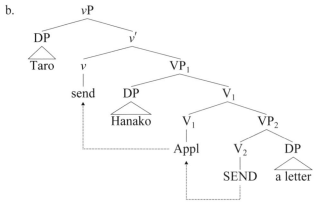

(Yasuhara and Nishimaki (2015: 587), with slight modifications))

In (77b), V_2 cyclically head-moves into Appl, which is hosted in V_1, and v. In English, a syntax-preferring language, conflation is adopted. As a result, Appl is covertly realized and the output of this head-movement appears as the simplex verb *to send*. On the other hand, the derivation of the *ageru* construction in (78a) is assumed to proceed as in (78b).

(78) a. Taro-ga   Hanako-ni   tegami-o   okutte-age-ta.   (= (74b))
    Taro-Nom Hanako-Dat letter-Acc send-Appl-Past
    'Taro sent Hanako a letter.'

b.

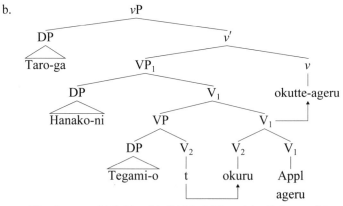

(Yasuhara and Nishimaki (2015: 588), with slight modifications))

Just like (77b), (78b) has the cyclic head-movement of V_2 into V_1 and v. However, in Japanese, a morphology-preferring language, the head-movement

Chapter 4   Further Applications   105

involved is incorporation. Consequently, Appl is overtly realized as *ageru* to form the compound *okutte-ageru* 'lit. to send-give = to send' (see Okura (2011) for an analysis of *ageru* 'to give' as an overt realization of Appl). The compoundhood of complex predicates such as *okutte-ageru* is confirmed by their conformity with the LIP. For example, they disallow intervening adverbials:

(79)   Taro-ga   Hanako-ni   tegami-o   okutte (*kyoo)   age-ta.
      Taro-Nom Hanako-Dat letter-Acc send   today Appl-Past
      'Taro sent Hanako a letter, today.'

In (79), the intervening *kyoo* 'today' yields an ungrammatical sentence or deprives the sentence of the intended reading.

    We can observe that the present analysis is applicable to the following translation pair:

(80)   a.   I baked him a cake.   (Pylkkänen (2008: 11))
      b.   Watasi-wa kare-ni   keeki-o   yaite-age-ta.
           I-Top   him-Dat cake-Acc bake-Appl-Past
           'I baked him a cake.'

(80a) illustrates so-called benefactive DOCs in English. Here again, they correspond to *ageru* constructions in Japanese, as shown in (80b). Typically, benefactive DOCs concern creation verbs, e.g. *to bake*. It can be seen that Japanese creation verbs, e.g. *yaku* 'to bake,' are incompatible with dative indirect objects, e.g. *kare-ni* 'him,' as shown in (81).

(81)   Watasi-wa (??kare-ni) keeki-o   yai-ta.
      I-Top   him-Dat cake-Acc bake-Past
      'I baked (??him) a cake.'

Confirmation for this correspondence is found in benefactive DOCs and *ageru* constructions exhibiting the defining property of DOCs: they require possessor DPs as indirect objects. For instance, because of this requirement, both constructions reject inanimate indirect objects, e.g. *table*, which cannot be construed as possessors:

(82)   a.   *I found the table a cloth.   (Green (1974: 104))
      b.   *Watasi-wa sono teeburu-ni teeburu-kake-o   mitukete-age-ta.
           I-Top   the   table-Dat   table-cloth-Acc find-Appl-Past

106   *A Study on Cross-Linguistic Variations in Realization Patterns*

The point is that English benefactive DOCs involve simplex verbs, e.g. *to bake*, but their corresponding *ageru* constructions in Japanese involve complex predicates, e.g. *yaite-ageru* 'lit. to bake-give = to bake.' Given this simplex-complex distinction, the present analysis tells us that benefactive DOCs and their corresponding *ageru* constructions derive via conflation and incorporation, respectively. Furthermore, it is confirmed that the relevant complex predicates take compound forms because they conform with the LIP, for example, to disallow intervening adverbials, e.g. *kyoo* 'today':[15]

(83) Watasi-wa kare-ni keeki-o yaite (*kyoo) age-ta.
      I-Top   him-Dat cake-Acc bake   today Appl-Past
      'I baked him a cake, today.'

In the standard view within the Minimalist Program, there is a functional head introducing agentive arguments, which are realized as subjects in overt syntax. This functional head is labeled as v by Chomsky (1995) or as Voice by Kratzer (1996). This v/Voice head is parallel with the Appl head in that both function to introduce external arguments into VP domains. This parallelism leads us to the expectation that v/Voice exhibits cross-linguistic variations in realization patterns in the same way as Appl. That is, it is predicted that syntax-preferring languages realize a structure projected by v/Voice as simplex verbs by means of conflation, whereas morphology-preferring languages realize the same structure as compounds through incorporation. The analysis in the literature on unergative verbs confirms that this is the case. These verbs are one-place predicates requiring agentive arguments. Therefore, they necessarily involve v/Voice. With this in mind, let us look at how unergatives are analyzed in English and Japanese.

---

[15] The present analysis can also apply to different realization patterns of directed motion constructions (see Zubizarreta and Oh (2007)) in English and Japanese, which are illustrated in the following translation pair:

(i) a. John walked to the station.
     b. John-ga   eki-ni   aruite-it-ta.
         John-Nom station-Loc walk-go-Past
         'John walked to the station.'

The point is that a motion verb like *to go* is covert in English while it is overtly realized as *iku* 'to go' in Japanese. See Yasuhara and Nishimaki (2017) for a competition-theoretic analysis of directed motion constructions.

In Section 4.4.1, we observed that in Hale and Keyser's (1993, 1997, 1998, 2002, 2005) analysis English unergatives derive through the conflation of nouns into a covert light verb:

(84) a. The children laughed.
 b.

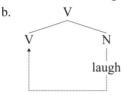

(= (60))

As predicted, Japanese counterparts of English simplex unergatives are compounds, which are as highly productive as English unergatives. We can find the following examples in Chunagon Corpus:

(85) dooi-suru 'to agree'; esyaku-suru 'to greet'; geketu-suru 'to flux'; gookyuu-suru 'to moan'; hitooyogi-suru 'to have a swim'; inemuri-suru 'to nap'; kenka-suru 'to fight'; kobasiri-suru 'to trot '; kooron-suru 'to quarrel'; nokku-suru 'to knock'; oetu-suru 'to weep'; ooto-suru 'to vomit'; ronsoo-suru 'to argue'; roodoo-suru 'to work'; sanpo-suru 'to walk'; sukkipu-suru 'to skip'; takawarai-suru 'to guffaw'; tyoosyoo-suru 'to ridicule'; tyooyaku-suru 'to jump'; zatudan-suru 'to chat'; zekkyoo-suru 'to scream'; zyanpu-suru 'to jump'

As shown in these examples, Japanese unergative compounds are characteristically headed by the light verb *suru* 'to do,' whose English counterpart is covert. The compoundhood of the expressions given in (85) is corroborated by their conformity to the LIP. For example, they disallow partial deletion by gapping:

(86) A-wa nokku*(-si), B-wa esyaku-si-ta.
 A-Top knock*(-do) B-Top greet-do-Past
 'A knocked and B greeted.'

In this example, the deletion of the first *-si* (i.e. the *renyoo* form of *suru* 'to do') by gapping results in ungrammaticality. Kageyama (1993: Ch. 5) and Saito and Hoshi (2000), among others, analyze these compounds as resulting

108   *A Study on Cross-Linguistic Variations in Realization Patterns*

from noun incorporation. For example, in the unergative *sanpo-suru* 'to walk,' the (verbal) noun *sanpo* 'walk' incorporates into *suru*. Interestingly, polysynthetic languages realize unergatives as incorporated compounds in the same way as Japanese. This is illustrated by the following data from the Tanoan languages, polysynthetic languages spoken in Arizona and New Mexico, which are originally mentioned by Hale and Keyser (1998: 114-115):

(87) a.   sae-'a   'to work'
           work-do
     b.   se-'a   'to speak'
           speech-do
     c.   shil-'a   'to cry'
           cry-do
     d.   zaae-'a   'to sing'
           song-do

(Hale and Keyser (1998: 115))

In these unergative N-V compounds, nouns incorporate into the overt light verb *'a* 'to do.'

Here, we would like to return to resultative constructions. In Section 4.2.1, we confirmed that English and Japanese realize these constructions in such a way that their realization patterns reflect the distinction between syntax-preferring and morphology-preferring languages. In addition to realization patterns, the license of resultative constructions differs between English and Japanese, reflecting the macroparametric distinction. Under Competition Theory, this difference can also be captured as the conflation-incorporation distinction, if we adopt the licensing mechanism proposed by Hasegawa (1999). Assuming that resultative predicates make their own projections, Hasegawa proposes that resultative constructions are licensed if heads of the relevant projections move into V; and this head movement yields accomplishment eventualities.

Based on this proposal, the English resultative constructions in (88a) and (88b), which involve a strong and a weak resultative, respectively, can be analyzed as in (88c) (where, adopting Hasegawa's (1999) notation, we symbolize the node hosting resultative predicate projections as VrP and the terminal node heading these projections as Vr).

(88) a. Hanako pounded the metal flat. (= (9a))
b. Mary dyed the dress pink. (= (5))
c.
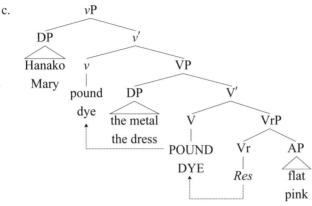

According to Hasegawa (1999: 196), English has the abstract predicate *Res* under Vr; this predicate moves into V and *v* to form a verbal complex. Given that this verbal complex is realized as a simplex verb such as *to pound*, our analysis suggests that the head movement involved is conflation, as required by Competition Theory.

We turn to consider how Japanese RVVCs, which realize strong resultatives, can be derived from their underlying structures. The RVVC in (89a) can be analyzed as in (89b).

(89) a. Hanako-ga   kinzoku-o   (taira-ni)   tataki-nobasi-ta.
      Hanako-Nom metal-Acc   (flat)   pound-spread-Past
      'Hanako pounded the metal flat.' (= (9b))
b.
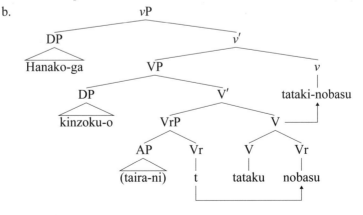

110   *A Study on Cross-Linguistic Variations in Realization Patterns*

Hasegawa (1999: 197) points out that there is no abstract predicate *Res* in Japanese, in which change-of-state verbs instead have a function similar to that of *Res*. In (89b), the change-of-state verb *nobasu* 'to spread' incorporates with the activity verb *tataku* 'to pound' to form the RVVC *tataki-nobasu* 'lit. to pound-spread = to pound,' as predicted by the present analysis. Because of its incorporated status, V and Vr are overtly realized by separate morphemes.[16] Hasegawa (1999) draws the generalization that abstract predicate *Res* exists in some languages, e.g. English, and not in others, e.g. Japanese. While Vr is abstract in English, it hosts a lexical item, i.e. a change-of-state verb, in Japanese. Under the present analysis, this descriptive generalization is amenable to a principled explanation: the 'abstract-lexical' distinction comes from the conflation-incorporation distinction, which reflects the distinction between syntax-preferring and morphology-preferring languages.

As discussed in Section 4.2.1, in order to capture their marked phrasal realization, we assume that Japanese weak resultatives have the functional Pred. For example, the weak resultative in (90a) has the underlying structure illustrated in (90b).

(90) a.   John-wa   pankizi-o   usu-ku nobasi-ta.
          John-Top dough-Acc   thin   roll.out-Past
          'John rolled the dough thin.'

---

[16] Two additional comments are in order. First, the incorporation analysis of Japanese RVVCs given in (89b) means that they constitute a natural class with so-called syntactic compounds, e.g. *tabe-hazimeru* 'lit. to eat-begin = to begin to eat.' However, given their semi-productivity and idiosyncrasies, one might suspect that RVVCs are classified into so-called lexical compounds, whose derivation involves no head movement (see Kageyama (1993, 2009) for the distinction between syntactic and lexical compounds). Since the discussion on whether RVVCs are syntactic or lexical is beyond the scope of the present analysis, we do not go into further details. For the discussion on this issue, see Nishiyama (1998) and Hasegawa (1999). In favor of the incorporation analysis of RVVCs, these authors explain their semi-productivity, idiosyncrasies, and so on. Second, one might wonder why in (89b) *nobasu* 'to spread' is right-adjoined given that incorporation (head-movement) normally results in left-adjoined configurations (see Baker (1996)). Hasegawa (1999: 294–295) attributes this right-adjoined configuration to the requirement of the Temporal Iconicity Condition (TIC), which specifies that predicates should be arranged in the 'cause-result' liner order (see Section 4.2.1). Optimality-theoretically, in the case of RVVCs, the semantico-conceptual constraint TIC overrides the syntactic constraint of the default left-adjoined configuration.

b.

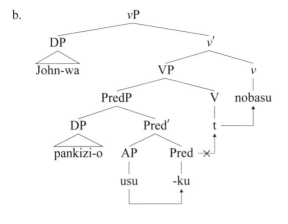

(= (16))

In this configuration, we take Pred as equivalent to Vr. The presence of Pred prevents adjectival stems from incorporating into V to form compounds, which results in phrasal realization of Japanese weak resultatives.[17]

Our discussion so far may suggest that Japanese uses incorporation to realize counterparts of English locative verbs, e.g. *to shelve*, as compounds. But this is not the case; the Japanese counterparts in question have phrasal realization.[18] This phrasal realization can be given the same explanation that

---

[17] Under the present analysis, the eventuality that verbs express and the state that resultative predicates represent are not connected in Japanese weak resultatives because the head-movement of Pred to V does not take place. What is predictable from this fact is that the accomplishment eventuality is not necessarily ensured in Japanese weak resultatives. In fact, Ono (2007: 22–23) points out that they do not express the accomplishment eventuality as clearly as English weak resultatives do:

(i) a. Kare-wa naya-o   itiniti-zyuu   penki-de aka-ku nut-ta.
       he-Top barn-Acc one.day-throughout paint-with red-Pred paint-Past
       'He painted the barn red throughout the day.'
                                                            (Ono (2007: 23))
    b. *He painted the car a brilliant red for an hour.   (Tenny (1994: 153))

A Japanese weak resultative does not necessarily force a telic reading, as shown by the compatibility with a durative time adverbial in (ia). Therefore, if the present analysis is on the right track, it may be that Japanese weak resultatives do not denote resultative meanings in a true sense unlike English ones; their resultative-like meanings pragmatically arise, as pointed out by Nitta (2002), Kato (2007), Imoto (2009), Miyakoshi (2012), and Takahashi (2013a, b), among others. Thus, this difference between English and Japanese weak resultatives can be nicely captured by the present analysis.

[18] Sugiok and Kobayashi (2001: 246) point to the possibility that English locative verbs

we provide for that of Japanese weak resultatives. If we adopt Hale and Keyser's (1993, 1997, 1998, 2002, 2005) analysis of locative verbs, the Japanese locative expression in (91a) can be analyzed as in (91b).

(91) a. John-wa tana-ni hon-o oi-ta.
John-Top shelf-on book-Acc put-Past
'John shelved the books / John put the books on a shelf.'

b.

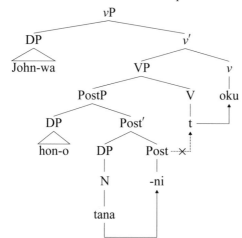

In this configuration, the existence of Post(position) is crucial. Recall from Chapter 3, Section 3.2.2, that Baker (2003a: Appendix) analyzes adpositions as functional heads. Given this, the incorporation of N through Post into V induces the violation of the PHMG, which is given in (92), because the intermediate Post is functional.

(92) A lexical head A cannot move to a functional head B and then to a lexical head C. (= (17))

Interestingly, polysynthetic languages also lack incorporated compounds corresponding to locative verbs. For example, Baker (1996, 2003a) observes that Mohawk never allows the combination of a noun plus a locative adposition to

---

may correspond to Japanese N-V compounds illustrated in (i).

(i) bin-zume(-suru) 'to bottle'; hako-zume(-suru) 'to box'; hukuro-zume(-suru) 'to bag'; syako-ire(-suru) 'to garage'; tana-age(-suru) 'to shelve'

We leave this possibility open. Nevertheless, we speculate that these N-V compounds differ in underling structure from English locative verbs and involve no incorporation.

incorporate into a verb:

(93) *Wa-k-atekhwara-hné-hrΛ-'.
FACT-IsS-table-LOC-put-PUNC
'I put it on the table.'

(Baker (1996: 430))

This lack can be explained in the same way. In this case, the movement from *hné* 'on' into the verb *hrΛ* 'to put' results in the violation of the PHMG.

Given our observation of verbal domains, we can safely conclude that English and Japanese contrast in selecting simplex or complex forms and that this contrast can be described as reflecting the conflation-incorporation distinction. Note that we draw the same conclusion from the observation of adpositions. Hale and Keyser (2002: 79–88) and Baker (2003a: Appendix) point out that lexical prepositions, e.g. *under*, in English derive if location-denoting relational nouns conflate into covert functional prepositions (for the distinction between lexical and functional adpositions, see Beard (1995: 247) and Svenonius (2006)). According to these authors, for instance, the functional PP *at the table* and the lexical PP *under the table* can be analyzed as in (94a) and (94b), respectively.

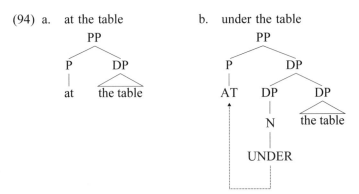

In (94b), P selects DP as its complement, which is composed of the relational noun UNDER and the DP complement *the table*. UNDER conflates into the covert AT, which is hosted in P, to surface as the lexical preposition *under*. Its nominal status is corroborated by the fact that the lexical preposition can serve as a subject, as in (95a), or an object, as in (95b).

(95) a. Under the elm is a nice place for a picnic.

   b. I prefer under the maple.

(Baker (2003a: 305-304, fn. 1))

Under the present analysis, the covert functional prepositions mean that lexical prepositions in English take simplex forms. Interestingly, Hale and Keyser (2002: 86) suggest that such underlying structures as those given in (94b) are realized in phrasal forms, such as *on top of*, *at the side of*, and *at the rear of*, if these structures do not undergo conflation. This situation is parallel to that found in conflated simplex verbs like unergatives (*to laugh* vs. *to have a laugh*).

On the other hand, as Hawkins (1993: 341) and Snyder (2012: 295) observe, Japanese lacks postpositions equivalent to English lexical prepositions; instead, their Japanese counterparts are relational nouns (e.g. *usiro* 'behind' and *sita* 'under') followed by postpositions (e.g. *-de* 'at' and *-ni* 'to'). The following examples show that the Japanese *usiro-de* and *sita-ni* correspond to the English lexical prepositions *behind* and *under*, respectively:

(96) a. Neko-ga hako-no usiro-de ne-te-imasu.

   cat-Nom box-Gen behind-at sleep-Prog-be.Polite

   'The cat is sleeping behind the box.'

(Hawkins (1993: 342))

   b. Neko-wa teeburu-no sita-ni it-ta.

   cat-Top table-Gen under-to go-Past

   'The cat went under the table.'

(Snyder (2012: 295))

The standard analysis suggests that combinations like *usiro-de* 'behind' and *sita-ni* 'under' are postpositional phrases and that they are, thus, irrelevant to incorporation (see Miyagawa (1989) and Tsujimura (2007)). Nevertheless, given that their English counterparts derive via conflation, the present analysis strongly suggests that they involve incorporation and have lexical status. If so, such combinations as *usiro-de* and *sita-ni* may be analyzed as follows:

(97)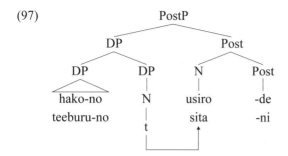

As with lexical prepositions, Post(position) selects DP complements headed by relational nouns, which are incorporated into Post. Although this possibility must be explored with great care, we have some motivations for the present analysis. For example, the configuration given in (97) strands the genitive NPs *hako-no* 'box's' and *teeburu-no* 'table's.' Hale and Keyser (2002: 60) point out that the stranding is specific to (noun) incorporation and impossible in conflation. Another motivation is Baker's (1988, 1996) observation that noun incorporation into adpositions is widely attested in polysynthetic languages. In particular, Baker (1996: 405) points out that Mohawk obligatorily requires incorporation to shift nouns and their governing prepositions into lexical units, as illustrated in (98) (where the following abbreviations are used: DU = dualic, N = neuter gender, PRE = nominal inflection prefix):

(98) ... o'k' tcinōwę' e'   t-oň-tke'totę'   o-ner-a'tōkǫ'.
     just mouse   there DU-3N-peeked PRE-leaf-among
     'A mouse peeked up there among the leaves.'

(Baker (1988: 90))

In this example, the noun *ner* 'leaf' incorporates into the preposition *a'tōkǫ'* 'among' to form the lexical unit *o-ner-a'tōkǫ'* 'lit. leaf-among.' If the present analysis is on the right track, the lack of lexical adposition in Japanese is attributable to the fact that conflation is a marked option in Japanese because it is a morphology-preferring language.

4.5. Summary

This chapter has observed that the distinction between a syntax-preferring and a morphology-preferring language manifests itself in various ways, focusing on English and Japanese. This distinction can appear between two forms: phrases and compounds, free and bound forms, and simplex and complex forms. It is also apparent between two operations: conflation and incorporation. Under Competition Theory, these distinctions all result from the single macroparameter that determines whether syntactic or morphological realization is selected as a default option in a given language. In this sense, the various contrasts between English and Japanese observed in this chapter are all parallel, whether they involve phrase-compound, free-bound, simplex-complex, or conflation-incorporation distinctions. Phrasal, free, and simplex forms and conflation all serve for syntactic realization or minimizing of morphological complexity. On the other hand, compound, bound, and complex forms and incorporation are all used for morphological realization or syntactic-complexity minimizing. Our exploration has demonstrated that a competition-theoretic approach can give a unified treatment of cross-constructional as well as cross-linguistic variations, which have been separately discussed in the literature. It can ultimately, then, derive descriptive generalizations or typological differences from macroparametric properties of languages.

Chapter 5

Conclusion

This thesis has pursed possibilities of a competition-theoretic approach to cross-linguistic variations. Competition Theory, along the lines of generative perspectives on human language, assumes that there is no difference among particular languages on an abstract level, and that their variations merely reside in externalization, that is, how the common abstract structure is realized. Specifically, whether morphological realization or syntactic realization is available is macroparametrically determined for a particular language.

Our inquiry in this thesis has revealed that a competition-theoretic approach provides a new perspective on cross-linguistic variations and provides an interesting twist to the study of cross-linguistic universals and variations. For example, in the literature, it has been assumed that direct modification and strong resultatives are unattested in Japanese. However, the truth is that they really exist in the form of compounds even in Japanese, as required by its macroparametric value. Competition Theory tells us that the underlying structure of direct modification and strong resultatives is available in any language but their realization forms show morphology-syntax variations. Thus, a competition-theoretic approach can give a unified treatment of cross-linguistic and syntax-morphology variations. Also, cross-constructional variations can be given a unified treatment by adopting a competition-theoretic approach. This is illustrated in our treatment of A-N compounds and dvandvas. These compounds are parallel in that both are morphologically-realized forms of the direct merger of lexical items; the difference lies in whether the structures involved are asymmetrically headed or coordinated.

Our findings on contrastive realization patterns between English and Japanese are summarized in the following tables:

Table 7   Phrases vs. Compounds

	English (Phrases)	Japanese (Compounds)
Predicate · Argument	to wash cars	sen-sya(-suru)
Nominal Modification	òld fámily	kyuu-ka
Resultative Construction	to pound X flat	tataki-nobasu (lit. to pound-spread)
Aspectual Verb Particle Construction	to drink X up	nomi-hosu (lit. to drink-exhaust)
Directional Verb Particle Construction	to take X back	moti-kaeru (lit. to take-return)
'Time'-*Away* Construction	to drink X away	nomi-akasu (lit. to drink-pass)
Body Part Off Construction	to talk one's head off	syaberi-makuru (lit. to talk-turn.up)
Coordination	husband and wife	huu-hu

(= Table 2 in Chapter 2)

Chapter 5 Conclusion 119

Table 8 Free Forms vs. Bound Forms

	English (Free Forms)	Japanese (Bound Forms)
Speech Act		
One-Sided Information Giving	It is raining, I tell you.	Ame-da yo.
Confirmation to the Hearer	It is raining, you know.	Ame-da ne.
Request for Hearer's Agreement	John left, didn't he?	John-wa dekake-masi-ta ne.
Interrogative	What did Mary buy?	Mary-ga nani-o kai-masi-ta ka.
Evidentiality		
Hearsay	I hear Mary won the prize.	Mary-ga syoo-o totta tte.
Direct Evidentiality	Into the room came John.	Heya-ni haitte kitano-wa John-da Ø.
Indirect Evidentiality	It seems that a fire is occurring.	Kazi-da na.

Table 9 Conflation / Simplex Forms vs. Incorporation / Complex Forms

	English (Conflation / Simplex Forms)	Japanese (Incorporation / Complex Forms)
Double Object Construction	to send	okutte-ageru (lit. to send-give)
Benefactive Double Object Construction	to bake	yaite-ageru (lit. to bake-give)
Unergative Construction	to walk	sanpo-suru (lit. to walk-do)
Adposition	under	sita-ni (lit. under-at)

120　*A Study on Cross-Linguistic Variations in Realization Patterns*

The point is that these contrasts all result from the single macroparameter that determines whether syntactic or morphological realization is selected. In some cases, the macroparametric distinction between English and Japanese may surface as the phrase-compound distinction; in other cases it may appear as the free-bound or simplex-complex distinction. Thus, a competition-theoretic approach works well in describing these different types of contrasts as parallel phenomena.

Importantly, in Competition Theory, morphological realization and syntactic realization are never regulated by inviolable rules, as the terminologies 'syntax-preferring languages' and 'morphology-preferring languages' suggest. If there is no competition between syntactic and morphological realizations, the remaining non-default option is selected, as illustrated in the following examples:

(1)　Morphologically-Realized Forms in English: Embedded Compounds
    a.　[[truck drive]-er / -ing]
    b.　[[blue-eye]-ed] ('having a blue eye / blue eyes')
                                    (= (15) in Chapter 3)
    c　a *ten-year-old* girl   (= (12a) in Chapter 2)
    d.　the *Balkan-weary* troops   (= (12b) in Chapter 2)
    e.　*doctor-patient* dialogue   (= (12c) in Chapter 2)

(2)　Syntactically-Realized Forms in Japanese
    a.　{aoi　garasu-no　/ ?*garasu-no　aoi} koppu
       blue glass-Linker /　glass-Linker blue　glass
      'blue glass glass'
                                   (= (17a) in Chapter 3)
    b.　John-wa　pankizi-o　usu-ku nobasi-ta.
      John-Top dough-Acc thin　　roll.out-Past
      'John rolled the dough thin.'
                                   (= (90a) in Chapter 4))
    c.　John-wa　tana-ni　hon-o　　oi-ta.
      John-Top shelf-on book-Acc　put-Past
      'John shelved books. / John put the books on a shelf.'
                                   (= (91a) in Chapter 4))

Thus, Competition Theory can provide a unified treatment of these marked realization patterns as well as unmarked ones.

Chapter 5 Conclusion   121

Furthermore, a competition-theoretic approach can open up a new perspective on the treatment of the forms and operations listed in Tables 7–9. They can be characterized as options either for syntactic realization / morphological-complexity minimizing or morphological realization / syntactic-complexity minimizing. Based on this characterization, the above forms and operations are classified as follows:

Table 10   Competition-Theoretic Characterization of Forms and Operations

Syntactic Realization / Morphological-Complexity Minimizing	Morphological Realization / Syntactic-Complexity Minimizing
Forms	
Phrasal	Compound
Free	Bound
Simplex	Complex
Operations	
Phrase Formation	Compounding
Conflation	Incorporation

These are parameterized options: whether the options given in the left or right column are used by default is parametrically determined for a given language.

Our cross-linguistic research in this thesis has demonstrated that Competition Theory can nicely characterize English as a syntax-preferring language and Japanese and polysynthetic languages as morphology-preferring languages. Finally, in order to provide an outlook for future research, we would like to give a brief sketch of other languages within the framework of Competition Theory. As a first example, let us take Romance languages. Talmy's (1985, 1991, 2000) influential verb-framed and satellite-framed typology classifies these languages and Japanese into the same group but English into another group.[1] However, we assume that they fall into the group of

---

[1] Note that Talmy's verb- and satellite-framed typology is in fact sensitive only to the difference in surface realization. See Snyder (2012: 279–281) and Yasuhara and Nishimaki (2017) on the fundamental distinction between this type of typology and our parametric approach to cross-linguistic variations.

syntax-preferring languages like English. This assumption is motivated by the observation that N-N and A-N compounds have little productivity in Romance languages and expressions that may be regarded as compounds are in fact lexicalized phrases. Based on this observation, Di Sciullo and Williams (1987: 83) states that "[i]t now appears that French (and no doubt Spanish) lacks compounding altogether" (also see Zwanenburg (1992); Snyder (1995, 2001, 2012); Booij (2002b); Fradin (2009)). In addition, dvandvas are unattested in Romance languages (e.g. Bauer (2008), Arcodia et al. (2010)). Also, they have weak resultatives in phrasal forms, though they lack strong resultatives (see Napoli (1992)). Turning to other European languages, Modern Greek is interesting. It is likely that this language is a morphology-preferring language. This is because exceptionally among European languages dvandvas are attested in Modern Greek; and other types of compounds are very productive (e.g. Ralli (1992, 2008, 2009), Arcodia et al. (2010)). Note also that it is a typical example of a stem-based language, which makes much use of bound stems for compounding. Regarding Asian languages, Mandarin Chinese and Korean may be taken as morphology-preferring languages, because various types of compounds, including V-V compounds and dvandvas, are widely observed (for Mandarin Chinese see Ceccagno and Basciano (2009) and for Korean see Tsukamoto (2012)).

Appendix*

Lexicalization Analysis of English 'Root Compounds' and Related Issues

1. Introduction

Competition Theory views compounding as an option for morphological realization, which entails the definition of compounds as morphologically-realized forms of the merger of lexical items. In this view, we have hold that English, i.e. a syntax-preferring language, has synthetic but not root compounds (e.g. *truck driver / truck driving* vs. *ballot box*). This is because the merger of lexical items in syntax-preferring languages results in phrasal realization, which blocks compound realization, unless some special factor prevents the morphology-syntax competition. Synthetic compounds are allowed even in English, because selectional restrictions on the agentive *-er* and the gerundive *-ing* involved prevent the morphology-syntax competition. In contrast, root compounds are impossible in English because nothing suspends this competition; by definition, these compounds do not have the suffixes *-er* and

---

* An earlier version of this appendix was presented at the meeting of Morphology Days 2015 held at the University of Leuven, Belgium, on December 17–18, 2015. For many stimulating and rewarding discussions on an earlier version of this appendix, I am indebted to Yukio Hirose, Nobuhiro Kaga, Masaharu Shimada, Naoaki Wada, Masaru Kanetani, and Akiko Nagano.

124 *A Study on Cross-Linguistic Variations in Realization Patterns*

-*ing*. In Chapter 2, Section 2.4.1, following the lexicalization analysis proposed in the literature, we argued that putative root compounds in English are not compounds in a true sense but lexicalized phrases: specifically, they are generated as syntactic phrases and enter into the lexicon, which results in their accidental acquisition of lexical properties. This appendix explores this lexicalization analysis to further corroborate our assumption that English has no root compound. Our exploration demonstrates that expressions alleged to be root compounds in English are inherently syntactic phrases, some of which may undergo lexicalization to look as if they were compounds.

The organization of this appendix is as follows. Section 2 defines lexicalization to clearly distinguish between this process and compounding. Based on this definition, Section 3 proves the phrasal origins of alleged root compounds in English and their lexicalized status. Section 4 scrutinizes N-N combinations that look like synthetic compounds to identify them as attributive phrases. Section 5 looks at lexicalized phrases in other languages than English and examine cross-linguistic variations in lexicalization.

2. The Definition of Lexicalization and Compounding: Their Fundamental Difference

According to Brinton and Traugott (2005), the most broad definition of lexicalization is the listing of new items in the lexicon. Other common definitions of lexicalization are illustrated in the following:[1]

(1) a. [...] the integration of a word formation or syntactic construction into the lexicon with semantic and / or formal properties which are not completely derivable or predictable from the constituents or the pattern of formation.   (Kastovsky (1982: 164–165))

   b. [...] lexicalization is the process whereby independent, usually monomorphemic, words are formed from complex constructions

---

[1] (1a) is an English translation by Brinton and Traugott (2005: 56). The original German passage is the following:

   (i) [...] die Eingliederung eines Wortbildungs- oder syntaktischen Syntagmas in das Lexikon mit semantischen und / oder formalen Eigenschaften, die nicht vollständig aus den Konstituenten oder dem Bildungsmuster ableitbar sind.

[...] (Traugott (1994: 1485))

c. Lexicalization is the change from phrasal to lexical category status with concomitant loss of internal – morphological, phonological, semantic – structure. (Giegerich (2004: 14))

d. [...] lexicalization (like grammaticalization or constructionalization) is a gradual diachronic process [...]
(Rosenbach (2010: 169))

These definitions indicate that lexicalization has at least two necessary ingredients: the listing of complex items in the lexicon and the gradual loss of their internal structures. Brinton and Traugott (2005: 96) combine these two ingredients to define lexicalization as follows:

(2) Lexicalization is the change whereby in certain linguistic contexts speakers use a syntactic construction or word formation as a new contentful form with formal and semantic properties that are not completely derivable or predictable from the constituents of the construction or the word formation pattern. Over time there may be further loss of internal constituency and the item may become more lexical.

Adopting this definition, let us consider the difference between compounding and lexicalization in the discussion that follows.

Compounding and lexicalization are seemingly similar in that their outputs show lexicality. But a closer examination reveals that these processes are crucially different. Competition-theoretically, the most crucial difference lies in whether they involve structural realization or not. Compounding is a morphological option for structural realization whereas lexicalization is not responsible for this task. Therefore, the availability of lexicalization in a given language does not depend on whether it is a syntax-preferring or morphology-preferring language. In this sense, lexicalization is a language-neutral process; on the other hand, compounding is a language-sensitive process in that its use as a default option is restricted to morphology-preferring languages. This crucial difference has further implications. First, it entails different inputs. Inputs to compounding are underlying structures generated by Merge; on the other hand, inputs to lexicalization are realization forms of these structures. In this sense, lexicalization requires prior structural realization. Another implication is the difference between rule-governedness and randomness. Under Competition Theory, compounding is parameterized as an option for structural realization. In this sense, it is a rule-governed process. This rule-governedness leads us to the assumption that outputs, i.e. compounds, are uniform in behavior, including lexicality and endocentricity. In contrast, lexicalization can be taken as a random process, given that its necessary ingredient is listing, which is not rule-governed. Therefore, lexicalization "is non-instantaneous, and proceeds by very small and typically overlapping, intermediate, and sometimes indeterminate, steps (Brinton and Traugott (2005: 97))." As a result of this gradual nature, outputs show a degree of non-uniformity in behavior.

Our considerations so far are summarized as follows:

Table 11   Properties of Compounding and Lexicalization

	(i) Compounding	**(ii) Lexicalization**
It is a process of	structural realization	listing
The process is	language-sensitive	language-neutral
Inputs are	underlying structures generated by Merge	realization forms of underlying structures
The process occurs	prior to lexicalization	subsequent to compounding
The process is	rule-governed	random and gradual
Outputs exhibit	behavioral uniformity	behavioral non-uniformity

We can define compounding as having the properties given in Table 11 (i) and lexicalization as having those given in Table 11 (ii). Among these properties, we would like to focus on the last one, that is, the behavioral (non-)uniformity of outputs. By using this property as a criterion, we can determine whether a given item is a compound or a lexicalized expression; the former exhibits behavioral uniformity but the latter does not. In the following discussion, we show that alleged root compounds in English can be best analyzed as lexicalized phrases because they are not uniform in behavior.

Appendix   Lexicalization Analysis of English 'Root Compounds' and Related Issues   127

3.   Lexicalization Analysis of English 'Root Compounds'

3.1.   Non-uniformity of N-N and A-N 'Root Compounds'

Let us start our discussion with alleged N-N and A-N compounds. Whether English N-N and A-N combinations are syntactic phrases or root compounds has presented a controversial issue in the literature. A problem is that these combinations show non-uniformity in behavior with respect to the word-phrase distinction. Some combinations behave like words, others behave like phrases, and yet others show mixed behaviors with respect to the word-phrase distinction. This is illustrated in the following N-N and A-N combinations:

(3) a. *a hair-net and a mosquito one   (Giegerich (2004: 12))
     b. I wanted a sewing machine, but he bought a washing one.
                                                   (Bauer (1998: 77))
(4) a. *Is he a constitutional lawyer or a criminal one?
                                                   (Giegerich (2005: 580))
     b. Is this the medical building or the dental one?
                                                   (Giegerich (2005: 588))

These N-N and A-N combinations all have the lexical feature of left-hand stress, but the examples in (b) allow the syntactic operation of *pro*-one replacement in violation of the LIP.[2] Given this behavioral non-uniformity, it is safe to assume that they are lexicalized phrases and not compounds. In contrast, synthetic compounds uniformly behave as words across the criteria of compoundhood. For example, according to Giegerich (2004), synthetic compounds always place their main stress on left-hand nonheads and disallow syntactic operation, e.g. *pro*-one replacement (*a watch-maker and a cabinet one* (Giegerich (2004: 9))).

Another illustration of behavioral non-uniformity is the contrasting stress patterns in the following minimal pairs:

---

[2] Note that left-hand stress in (4) is not a matter of contrastive stress. According to Giegerich (2005: 588, fn. 15), the relevant A-N combinations have left-hand stress in their citation forms.

(5) a. Mádison Strèet   a'. Màdison Ávenue
    b. ápple càke   b'. àpple píe

(Lees (1960: 120))

One might wonder why the minimal pairs take left-hand stress with the heads *street* and *cake* but right-hand stress with the heads *avenue* and *pie*. Such minimal pairs as those given in (5) display robust stress contrasts without any other difference in behavior. Since Lees (1960) pointed them out, these stress contrasts have defied a principled explanation, which means that stress patterns of the relevant nominals are not rule-governed but lexically conditioned. Lees (1960: 120) merely states that "all composites in -*street* and -*cake* are compounds, while all in -*avenue* and in -*pie* are invariably nominal phrases." Under the present analysis, this non-uniformity in stress pattern naturally follows from the lexicalized status; N-N combinations all originate in syntactic phrases while those having certain types of head nouns like *street* and *cake* are lexicalized to exhibit left-hand stress.

A stress pattern is a popular criterion to distinguish compounds from phrases. However, since Bloomfield (1933: 228) drew our attention to the variable stress patterns of *ice cream*, it has become well known that attributive N-N and A-N combinations are notoriously inconsistent in stress patterns. This can be readily understood if we compare stress markings in OED and two pronunciation dictionaries in the way that Bauer (1998: 70) does. The following tables indicate on which constituents, left or right, the three dictionaries mark main stress ('~' denotes variable stress patterns, and the spellings are those adopted in OED):

Appendix   Lexicalization Analysis of English 'Root Compounds' and Related Issues   129

Table 12   Stress Markings of N-N Combinations

Items	OED	Cambridge	Longman
apple pie	left~right	right	right
beef-steak	even	left~right	left
Christmas cake	no marking	left	left
Christmas-eve	no marking	right	right
city hall	right	right	right
city-state	left~right	not listed	right
cream-cheese	no marking	right	right
field hospital	no marking	left~right	not listed
field mouse	no marking	left	left
girlfriend	left	left	left
ice cream	even	left~right	right
master key	left~even	left	left~right
night school	left	left	left
nightwatch	left	left~right	left~right
oil well	left	left	left
peanut butter	left~right	right	left~right
potato chip	no marking	left	left
snowball	left	left	left
watermill	left	left	left
winter sport(s)	no marking	right	right

Table 13　Stress Markings of A-N Combinations

Items	OED	Cambridge	Longman
blackboard	left	left	left
blueprint	left	left	left
easy(-)chair	right~even	left	right
great-uncle	no marking	left~right	right
High Court	right	right	right
high pressure	right	right	right
high school	left	left	left
hot dog	left~right	left~right	right
hothouse	left	left	left
long distance	right	right	right
long wave	left	right	left~right
New Year	left~right	right	right
Old English	right	right	right
red cross	right	right	right
red meat	even	not listed	right
short wave	no marking	right	right
white-collar	right~even	left~right	right
white paper	right	left~right	right
white pepper	no marking	left~right	right
wide-angle	left~right	right	right

Observe that some combinations have lexical left-hand stress, others have phrasal right-hand stress, and yet others have even stress. Furthermore, different dictionaries may mark different patterns on the same combination. This inconsistency clearly confirms that N-N and A-N combinations undergo lexicalization at random to acquire lexical left-hand stress.

Liberman and Sproat (1992: 150–153) carefully distinguish three stages of lexicalization: semantic, syntactic, and morphophonemic lexicalization (also

Appendix   Lexicalization Analysis of English 'Root Compounds' and Related Issues   131

see Bauer (1983: Ch. 3)).[3] According to these authors, only in the final stage of morphophonemic lexicalization do lexicalized items come to be left-stressed. We can find this final stage in *háirnèt* or *bláckbòard*. In contrast, *ìce créam* or *Hìgh Cóurt* does not come to this stage. Accordingly, they retain their phrasal right-hand stress. The point is that *háirnèt, bláckbòard, ìce créam*, and *Hìgh Cóurt* all come from syntactic phrases, or rather syntactically-realized forms of attributive modification; the difference between *háirnèt / bláckbòard* and *ìce créam / Hìgh Cóurt* lies merely in the degree of lexicalization.

Competition-theoretically, such lexicalized N-N and A-N phrases as *háirnèt* and *bláckbòard* have the same status as the phrasal idioms illustrated in (6) in that they are all syntactically-realized forms of the merger of lexical items and listed in the lexicon for some reason.

(6)   AP (all wet), PP (in the dark about NP), S (the cat has got NP's tongue), N′ (that son of a bitch), NP (The Big Apple)

(Di Sciullo and Williams (1987: 6))

On the definition of idioms as listed syntactic units, Di Sciullo and Williams (1987: 6) argue that syntactic units of all kinds can be idioms. We agree with these authors that there is nothing special about N-N and A-N phrases.

The above discussion is sufficient to confirm that English N-N and A-N combinations are generated as syntactic phrases, some of which may be lexicalized to exhibit compound-like behaviors, e.g. left-hand stress placement; there are neither N-N nor A-N root compounds in English. Nevertheless, given the putative productivity, one might suspect that their derivation involves

---

[3] In semantic lexicalization, complex items are listed in the lexicon by acquiring non-compositional semantics. This first stage may induce syntactic lexicalization, in which category shift takes place on the listed items. For example, a listed NP may be relabeled as an N^0. In morphophonemic lexicalization, syntactically-lexicalized items may lose internal word boundaries. In other words, they are reanalyzed as monomorphemic words. Consequently, they become subject to phonological processes that would apply word-internally, which yields their lexical left-hand stress. Our assumption is that it is not until this final stage that listed items are so fully lexicalized as to strictly observe the LIP. Note that semantic lexicalization entails neither syntactic nor morphophonemic lexicalization: some items may finish their lexicalization at the first stage; and others may reach the final stage. Because of the randomness, it is impossible to predict the degree to which lexicalization proceeds in individual cases.

132   *A Study on Cross-Linguistic Variations in Realization Patterns*

the rule-governed process of compounding, as most researchers claim. The present analysis suggests that the productivity reflects that of syntactic phrases, which are possible inputs to lexicalization. Alternatively, it may be due to the fact that attributive N-N and A-N combinations are highly susceptible to lexicalization. According to Nagano (2013), syntactic attribution is structurally close to morphological concatenation. For example, as well known, syntactic attribution is structurally small in that the syntactic expansion of prenominal modifiers is restricted to some degree (see Williams (1982); Di Sciullo and Williams (1987); Sadler and Arnold (1994); Escribano (2004)). This can be seen from the fact that prenominal modifiers cannot select their complements (e.g. *a grateful for the present child* (Sadler and Arnold (1994: 189))). This structural smallness is reminiscent of compounding. Moreover, notice that as far as attributive modification is concerned syntax and morphology share a head position in English. Syntactic attributive modification is exceptionally head-final in English. This head-finalness is compatible with the Righthand Head Rule (RHR), which requires "the head of a morphologically complex word to be the righthand member of that word [...] (Williams (1981: 248))" We assume that this shared head position makes it easy to reanalyze attributive phrasal structures as lexical units. Plausibly, these factors contribute to the higher degree of susceptibility of phrasal attributive combinations to lexicalization.

It can be concluded from our discussion so far that N-N and A-N combinations in English have phrasal origin even though they may look like compounds as a result of lexicalization. The following subsection applies the lexicalization analysis to other types of combinations that may be treated as root compounds.

3.2. Other Cases of Lexicalized Phrases

Such genitive-noun combinations as those given in (7) may be referred to as 'genitive compounds,' because their main stresses are on left-hand genitives.

(7)   gírl's shcòol, bírd's nèst,ców's mìlk, cálves' lìver

(Quirk et al. (1985: 328))

In addition to lexical stress pattern, these 'genitive compounds' exhibit lexical

Appendix   Lexicalization Analysis of English 'Root Compounds' and Related Issues   133

integrity. For example, they cannot be divided by adjectives:

(8) *a bird's new nest (cf. a new bird's nest)   (Biber et al. (1999: 295))

Here, notice the difference between descriptive and possessive genitives (see Quirk et al. (1985); Alexiadou et al. (2007); Rosenbach (2007)). Unlike descriptive genitives, constituting 'genitive compounds,' possessive genitives head DPs (e.g. *John's new book* (Alexiadou et al. (2007: 548, fn. 2))), which is confirmed by the fact that descriptive genitives can occur with other determiners (e.g. *these woman's magazines* (Shimamura (2014: 102))) but possessive genitives cannot (e.g.*the John's books on the table* (Alexiadou et al. (2007: 549))). In keeping with Shimamura (1999), we argue that 'genitive compounds' result from the lexicalization of DPs headed by possessive genitives. If so, their non-uniformity in lexicality is predicted. This prediction is supported by the mismatch between stress pattern and lexical integrity. For example, Taylor (1996: 291) regards *wóman's màgazine* as a genitive compound, because of its left-hand stress. Nevertheless, we can insert adjectives into this combination, as shown in (9).

(9) a.   "I'm not averse to marriage but I don't believe I'll ever do it" the singer, 52, told Woman's Own magazine.   (BNC CBF)
    b.   The most important of these for Isabella was the English Woman's Domestic Magazine (EDM) [...]   (BNC GTA)
    c.   [...] the woman's popular American magazine *Good House-keeping* [...]
        (Brian McHale and Randall Stevenson, *The Edinburgh Companion to Twentieth-Century Literatures in English*)
                                            (my underlining)

Next, we turn to so-called exocentric compounds, which are illustrated in the following:

(10)   birdbrain, hunchback, paleface, redskin   (Marchand (1969: 14))

The exocentricity of these combinations is seen from the fact that, for example, *birdbrain* means not a brain but 'person having a birdbrain = stupid person (Marchand (1969: 13)).' Under the definition of compounding as a rule-governed process (see Section 2), we assume that genuine compounds have endocentric structures in conformity with the RHR (except for a few cases,

134　*A Study on Cross-Linguistic Variations in Realization Patterns*

e.g. coordinated compounds, as discussed in Chapter 4, Section 4.2.2). This assumption means that the above exocentric combinations are not compounds. These combinations are sometimes called bahuvrihi compounds because they denote possessors of something. Our claim is that they originate in attributive N-N and A-N phrases with endocentric structures. Furthermore, based on Booij (2002b: 143) and Scalise and Fábregas (2010: 125), among others, we assume that the exocentricity arises if a semantic process kwon as metonymy applies to endocentric nominal phrases. Metonymy is a semantic process in which "a part of an entity is used to refer to the whole entity (Booij (2002b: 143))." For instance, *redskin* refers to a certain type of person by mentioning a red skin characteristic of that person. This metonymy-based special semantics triggers the listing of nominal phrases in the lexicon. This listing may be followed by the loss of their internal word boundaries, which results in their lexical left-hand stress (see fn. 3). In fact, Allen (1978: 101–102) points out that bahuvrihi compounds can be best analyzed as lexicalized phrases. This author observes that nominal phrases do not necessarily acquire bahuvrihi semantics, as shown in the following contrast:

(11)　a.　He is a pale-face.　(cf. He has a pale face.)

　　　b.　*He is a red-nose.　(cf. He has a red nose.)

(Allen (1978: 102))

This contrast finds no principled explanation. That is, the acquisition of bahuvrihi semantics by nominal phrases is a mere accident. Plausibly, this reflects the randomness of lexicalization.

The same is true of VP-based exocentric combinations:

(12)　a.　cut-throat, kill-joy, pick-pocket

(Liberman and Sproat (1992: 146))

　　　b.　comeback, break-down, cutout, make-up, pickup

(Marchand (1969: 385))

We argue that these combinations are examples of lexicalized VPs.[4] The combinations given in (12a) denote "the agent who or which performs what is

---

[4] Such combinations as those illustrated in (12) may be analyzed as converted nouns from VPs. For the conversion analysis, see, for example, Plag (2003: 110); Ackema and Neeleman (2004: 158–159, 162); Nagano (2008: 85).

indicated by the predicate / object nexus of the formal basis (Marchand (1969: 380))." Their phrasal origins are clearly seen from their verb-object linear orders. What kind of VP comes to function as agentive nominals depends on the idiosyncrasies of items involved; it is impossible to explain why the VP *to pick one's pocket*, for instance, has been lexicalized into an agentive nominal while other potential candidates, e.g. *to pick one's bag*, have not. According to Marchand (1969: 381) and Miller (2014: 54), they arose under the influence of French in Middle English. Additionally, according to Miller (2014: 54) and Liberman and Sproat (1992: 145), they have attained little productivity in English.

The combinations given in (12b) originate in so-called verb particle constructions. They "denote an act or specific instance of what is expressed in the verbal phrase (Marchand (1969: 384))." Di Sciullo and Williams (1987: 87) point out that these combinations are best regarded as lexicalized VPs. Interestingly, Miller (2013) observes that they are not licensed when particles have literal aspectual meanings (in the following, the parenthesized *of*-phrases are interpreted as arguments):

(13) a. *an eat-up (of food) (cf. I ate up the food.)   (Miller (2013: 35))
    b. a smoke-up (*of cigars) 'notice that a student's work is not up to standard'   (Miller (2013: 36), with slight modifications)

This observation naturally follows from our lexicalization analysis: semantic lexicalization is a prerequisite for syntactic or morphophonemic lexicalization, which derives the relevant nominals (see fn. 3).

A final illustration of lexicalized phrases is what is called phrasal compounds, in which phrases serve as prenominal modifiers:

(14) a floor of a birdcage taste, over the fence gossip (Lieber (1992: 11))

In (14), the N' *floor of a birdcage* and the PP *over the fence* modify the heads *taste* and *gossip*, respectively. In this regard, phrasal nonheads have the same attributive function that nominal and adjectival nonheads have in N-N and A-N combinations. According to Lieber (1988, 1992), their compoundhood is confirmed by their syntactic inseparability:

(15) *a floor of a birdcage <u>salty</u> taste   (Lieber (1992: 13))

The existence of phrasal compounds leads Lieber (1988, 1992) to the claim that syntactic phrases can freely occur within root compounds. However, this claim is untenable. First, the occurrence is far from free, because not all phrases are allowed to occur as nonheads. Observe the following contrast, which is reducible to the difference between the similar words *fence* and *hedge*:

(16) over the {fence / *hedge} gossip   (Shimamura (2005: 64))

This contrast in a minimal pair means that the (non-)occurrence of a given phrase as a nonhead is lexically conditioned in an unpredictable way. Second, the wordhood is questionable because heads are separable from nonheads:

(17) The stew had a rather uniquely pungent, floor of a birdcage, salty
      taste.   (Sproat (1993: 248))

On the basis of similar facts, Kato and Kageyama (1998) argue that some phrasal compounds conform to the LIP, as Lieber (1988, 1992) claims, but others do not. The lexically-conditioned occurrence and the variation in separability strongly suggest that the truth is that syntactic attributions where phrases premodify nouns may be lexicalized to exhibit compound-like behaviors.

    Let us consider phrasal nonheads in more detail. Given the structural smallness of prenominal modifiers, which was observed in Section 3.1, it is questionable whether nonheads of phrasal compounds have phrasal status in a true sense. In fact, they exhibit syntactic opacity. For example, in (18), we cannot insert the adjective *lavish* into the prepositional nonhead *after-the-party*.

(18) an after-the-(*lavish)-party mess   (Shimamura (1986: 26))

Based on these considerations, we follow Burstein (1992) and Shimamura (1986, 2003, 2005) in assuming that the nonheads in question result from the lexicalization of phrases. Because of their lexicalized status, they are not uniform in lexicality. This is illustrated by the following mixed behavior:

(19) John$_i$ is anxious to learn about the over-his$_i$-(*clear)-head theory.

In (19), the prepositional nonhead *over-his-head* allows the inbound anaphora *his*, which is coreferential with *John*, but disallows the insertion of the adjective *clear*. In this respect, the nonhead in question is both phrasal and lexical.

Appendix   Lexicalization Analysis of English 'Root Compounds' and Related Issues   137

4.   Verbal N-N Combinations as Attributive Phrases

Finally, we would like to examine the status of the following N-N combinations:

(20)   soil conservation, office management, slum clearance

(Fabb (1984: 185))

For convenience, we refer to these combinations as verbal N-N combinations because of their deverbal heads. Normally, verbal N-N combinations are also treated as compounds. But the present analysis tells us that they are syntactically realized as phrases to undergo lexicalization. Their behavioral non-uniformity confirms their lexicalized status. For example, let us consider *tax evasion* and *consumer protection*. These verbal N-N combinations have lexical left-hand stress (*táx evasion* (Longman, s.v. *tax*); *cónsumer protèction* (Namiki (1985: 84))). Nevertheless, their phrasal behaviors can be observed in the following data:

(21) a.   [...], tax avoidance <u>and</u> evasion will tend to increase.

(Tom Rolfe, *Financial Accounting and Tax Principles*)

b.   [...] the whole reorganization has tax evasion <u>or</u> avoidance [...]

(Michael Lang, Pasquale Pistone, and Josef Schuch, *Introduction to European Tax Law on Direct Taxation*)

(22)   Consumer <u>financial</u> protection is also a timely subject.

(Steven Payson, *Public Economics in the United States*)

(my underlining)

In (21), *tax evasion* is divided by coordination. In (22), *consumer protection* allows the insertion of the adjective *financial*.

Note here that in verbal N-N combinations deverbal heads seem to establish a predicate-argument relationship with nonheads. In this respect, the combinations in question are similar to synthetic compounds. Given this similarity, one might suspect that verbal N-N combinations constitute a natural class with synthetic compounds (see Allen (1978); Selkirk (1982); Grimshaw (1990); Oshita (1995)). But the two types of nominal belong to totally different classes because they have different structures (see Marchand (1969); Roeper and Siegel (1979); Fabb (1984)). Recall from Chapter 2, Section

2.4.2, that Competition Theory necessarily leads us to analyze synthetic compounds as in (23a). On the other hand, we assume that verbal N-N combinations are analyzed as in (23b) because they are attributive phrases, where heads and nonheads are in a modifiee-modifier relationship in the same way as non-verbal N-N combinations, e.g. *ice cream*.

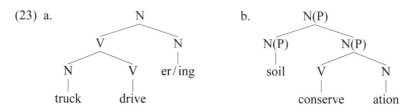

Our assumption is that the gerundive *-ing* and the agentive *-er* define synthetic compounds; their (non-)existence is responsible for this structural difference. This structural difference is corroborated by their striking behavioral differences. In what follows, let us examine these differences in detail.

The structural difference manifests itself as the difference as to the availability of certain types of dependent. In (23a), verbs satisfy their argument structures by merging with nouns within synthetic compounds. Due to these argument structures, synthetic compounds can occur with infinitival clauses, as shown in (24).

(24) city-destroying to prove a point   (Roeper (1987: 294))

This phenomenon is known as event control, which is licensed by verbal argument structures (see Roeper (1987) and Grimshaw (1990)). This being so, its possibility indicates that synthetic compounds inherit argument structures from their embedded verbs. Another fact indicating the inheritance of argument structures is that synthetic compounds allow second arguments:

(25) a. I've observed more than enough of your petty *doubt-casting on my management*.   (Morita (1998: 400))
   b. Mary cast doubt on John's management and *I did so, too / ??I did so on Mike's management*.   (Morita (1998: 401))

In (25a), the PP *on my management* functions to saturate the goal argument of the verb *to cast*. The status of the PP as an argument is corroborated by the

Appendix   Lexicalization Analysis of English 'Root Compounds' and Related Issues   139

impossibility of its occurrence outside the pro-form *do so*, as shown in (25b).[5]
On the other hand, verbal N-N combinations allow neither event control nor
second arguments:

(26) a. ?*city-destruction to prove a point   (Roeper (1987: 294))
     b. ??Her *money-expenditure on clothes* was so excessive that she was
        on the verge of bankruptcy.   (Morita (2003: 430))

This follows from the structure given in (23b), which is the merger of two
nouns and inherits no verbal argument structure.

Whether verbal argument structures are present yields the difference in
possible interpretation. The robust fact concerning English word formation is
that synthetic compounds, but not verbal N-N combinations, prohibit the interpretation of nonheads as external arguments, i.e. subjects (see Roeper and
Siegel (1979); Selkirk (1982); Fabb (1984)):

(27)   blood {circulation / *circulating}   (Fabb (1984: 186))
               ('*' with the nonhead *blood* interpreted as a subject)

We can interpret the nonhead *blood* as a subject in the verbal N-N combination *blood circulation* but not in the synthetic compound *blood circulating*.
This contrast tells us that the interpretation of verbal N-N combinations is not
regulated by the organization of verbal argument structures.

The structural analysis given in (23) shows that synthetic compounds and

---

[5] Agentive synthetic compounds allow neither event control nor second arguments, unlike
gerundive ones (see, for example, Sproat (1985); Roeper (1987); Oshita (1995)). Nevertheless, their inherited argument structures can be seen from their occurrence with temporal
modifiers, e.g. *frequent* and *constant*, which are normally assumed to be licensed by argument structures:

(i) a. [...] youngsters classified as <u>frequent</u> TV-watchers or cinema-goers are com-
         pared with demographically comparable children who watch TV or films less
         frequently.   (Albert R. Gilgen, *Contemporary Scientific Psychology*)
     b. The society had disciplinary rules and expelled any of its members who were
         <u>constant</u> trouble-makers in the home.
                                          (Kenneth Little, *West African Urbanization*)
                                                                    (my underlining)

We have no clear explanation for the behavioral difference between two types of synthetic
compound. However, we speculate that this difference may involve their different semantics. The agentive type denotes a person. In this respect, this type may be semantically
richer than the gerundive type, which describes abstract action.

140   *A Study on Cross-Linguistic Variations in Realization Patterns*

verbal N-N combinations differ as to whether verbs combine with suffixes to constitute nouns. In (23a), a verb and a suffix do not constitute any unit. Thus, verb-suffix strings in synthetic compounds are not independently existent (the following '&' denotes that the expressions in question are possible but happen to be non-existent):

(28)   & a breaker (cf. heartbreaker) / & the keeping (cf. house-keeping)

(Roeper and Siegel (1978: 219–220))

Further evidence for the non-constituency comes from the fact that synthetic compounds disallow the prefix *non-* to immediately precede the verb-suffix strings, as shown in (29a).

(29)   a.   *grain non-importer / *grain non-importing   (Fabb (1984: 187))

      b.   non-grain-importing   (Oishi (1988: 140))

Non- can attach to nouns, as shown in (29b). Given this selectional property, the strings *import-er* and *import-ing* in (29a) would be subject to *non-*prefixation, if they constituted nouns. Note that synthetic compounds allow the insertion of prefixes itself (e.g. *story-retelling* (Roeper and Siegel (1978: 218))). On the other hand, in (23b), a verb and a suffix combine to form a noun. Accordingly, in the case of verbal N-N combinations, deverbal heads can independently occur, as shown in (30a), and undergo *non-* prefixation, as shown in (30b).

(30)   a.   The examination was long.   (Grimshaw (1990: 49))

      a'.   The doctor's careful eye examination took a long time.

(Oshita (1995: 181))

      b.   grain non-importation   (Fabb (1984: 187))

Thus, it is natural that heads are modified as nouns in verbal N-N combinations. If so, it follows that nonheads serve as attributive modifiers in these combinations.[6] Their status as attributes is confirmed by their alternation with adjectives:

(31)   a.   Above all he restored the focus of music criticism onto the music

---

[6] As for the status of prenominal elements, Giegerich (2004: 4) states that "in the syntax, any pre-head dependent where the head is a noun must be an attribute."

Appendix Lexicalization Analysis of English 'Root Compounds' and Related Issues 141

itself. (BNC A1H)

a′. musical criticism 'act of criticizing music' (Levi (1978: 169))

b. It is also blamed on the human technologies of slaughter and environment destruction [...] (BNC H7K)

b′. Environmental destruction can occur at many points in the life of a product [...] (BNC HH3)

(my underlining)

From our discussion so far, we can naturally conclude that synthetic compounds and verbal N-N combinations are fundamentally different because of their different structures. The crucial difference is that verbal argument structures are involved in synthetic compounds but not in verbal N-N combinations. Certainly, the latter may permit the interpretation of nonheads as arguments of deverbal heads, but this interpretation does not come from verbal argument structures. As well known, in N-N combinations, "virtually any relation between head and nonhead is possible—within pragmatic limits, of course (Selkirk (1982: 23))." Given this, we assume that the argument-like interpretation arises pragmatically in verbal N-N combinations.

Recall here that the structural distinction between synthetic compounds and verbal N-N combination corresponds to that between -er / -ing and other nominalizing suffixes. A natural question is why this is so. It is reducible to the fact that these suffixes have essentially different status in syntax, if we follow Marchand (1969: 18–19), Fabb (1984: 189–190), and Nagano (2010) (also see Embick (2010: 44–58)). According to these authors, -er and -ing are pure category-changers while other nominalizers (e.g. -(at)ion, -ment, -al, -age, -th, and -ism) are naming suffixes. As a result, -er / -ing nominals and other derived nouns are treated differently in narrow syntax. Marchand (1969: 18) points out that -er / -ing nominals are transposed VPs. This means that these nominals count as VPs at any stage of syntactic derivation. It is not until the final stage (perhaps Spell-Out) that -er and -ing show up to shift VPs into nouns when grammatical contexts require them. In this sense, as pointed out by Fabb (1984: 190), these suffixes are inflectional rather than derivational. Therefore, argument structures can be inherited from VPs to synthetic compounds.[7] On the other hand, given that naming is the process that yields a

---

[7] Nishimaki (2018) observes that Possessional adjectives, e.g. *blue-eyed* (see Chapter 3,

142   *A Study on Cross-Linguistic Variations in Realization Patterns*

new name or label for an extralinguistic entity, it is safe to assume that derived nouns with naming suffixes are listed in the lexicon as such, as observed by Ito and Sugioka (2002: 80–81). Due to this listedness, they count as nouns from the Numeration to Spell-Out. Since they are nouns in nature, it is natural that they cannot have any verbal argument structure.[8]

5. Lexicalization as a Language-Neutral Process and Cross-Linguistic Variations

So far, we have observed that lexicalization may apply to syntactic phrases to yield compound-like expressions in English. As discussed in Section 2, lexicalization is a language-neutral process because it is not responsible for structural realization. Thus, this process can possibly take place in any language. In fact, lexicalized phrases are attested in Japanese as well as English. Some examples are given in (32) (the examples given in (32b) are quoted from *Sanseido's Shinmeikai Japanese Accent Dictionary* (Sanseido's Dictionary)).

(32) a.   akai hane (kyoodoo-bokin) 'Red Feather (Community Chest)';
          akai kien 'lit. red high spirits = women's high spirits'; kuroi kiri
          'lit. black fog = scandal associated with crime'; siroi tairiku 'lit.
          white continent = the Antarctic Continent' (Shimamura (2014: 20))
     b.   ama-no gawa 'lit. heaven's river = the Milky Way'; ama-no
          zyaku 'lit. heaven's devil = perverse person'; hati-no ko 'lit.
          bee's child = wasp larva'; hati-no su 'lit. bee's nest = hive'; ki-
          no me 'lit. tree's sprout = leaf bud'; mago-no te 'lit. grandson's
          hand = backscratcher'; take-no ko 'lit. bamboo's child = bamboo

---

Section 3.4.1.), are transposed NPs; these adjectives constitute a natural class with synthetic compounds and *-ed* is another instance of pure-category changers.

[8] Because of Grimshaw's (1990) influential analysis, it is a very popular view that derived nouns like *destruction* are complex event nominals. But the present analysis tells us that they cannot be complex event but result nominals, because they have no verbal argument structure. Within the framework of Distributed Morphology, Marantz (1997) and Embick (2010), among others, reach the same conclusion. We follow Marantz (1997) in assuming that their behaviors associated with complex event nominals come from mere pragmatic factors.

shoot'; umi-no ie 'lit. sea's house = seaside clubhouse'; umi-no sati 'lit. sea's happiness = marine products'; uo-no me 'lit. fish's eye = corn'

(32a) and (32b) exemplify lexicalized A-N phrases and NPs with genitives, respectively. As a result of lexicalization, they are pronounced with a lexical single accent. As with lexicalized phrases in English, those in Japanese show non-uniformity in behavior. This is illustrated by the following minimal pair (where '☐' denotes accent positions and ' · ' a pause in pronunciation):

(33) a.　a⎡ma-no⎤ gawa 'lit. heaven's river = the Milky Way'
　　 b.　⎡a⎤ma-no · ha⎡sidate⎤ 'lit. heaven's ladder (a place name)'

These two phrases are listed in Sanseido's Dictionary. In this sense, we can assume that they are both lexicalized. Nevertheless, the dictionary tells us that they are differently pronounced. As shown in (33a), *ama-no* 'heaven's' and *gawa* 'river' constitute a single accent unit with the right-hand noun voiced by *Rendaku* (/kawa/→/gawa/). In contrast, as shown in (33b), which retains a phrasal accent, *ama-no* 'heaven's' and *hasidate* 'ladder' are separately accented without *Rendaku*. In this behavioral non-uniformity, these lexicalized phrases contrast sharply with N-N and A-N compounds, which are rule-governed to exhibit a consistent compound account.

Note that the degree to which lexicalization is used may vary from language to language, depending on its morphosyntax, while the process is language-neural; it is likely that some languages make much use of lexicalization and others do not. For example, Akiko Nagano (personal communication) points out that Romance languages have much fewer lexicalized N-N phrases than English does (also see Basciano et al. (2011: 208)). We speculate that the difference in word order may explain this difference. In the case of attributive modification, English has a head-final syntactic structure, which is compatible with the RHR. In Section 3.1, we pointed to the possibility that this compatibility may promote attributive phrasal structures to be reanalyzed as lexical units. In contrast, Romance languages always require a head-initial syntactic structure, whether attributive modification is involved or not. Another illustration of cross-linguistic variations in lexicalization can be found in the *picket-pocket* type of agent nominals, which result from the lexicalization of VPs. This type has no productivity in English (see Section 3.2) but is

144 *A Study on Cross-Linguistic Variations in Realization Patterns*

widely observed in Romance languages:

(34) a. cuentachistes 'lit. tell jokes = joke teller'   (Spanish)
   b. rabat-joi 'lit. reduce joy = spoil sport'   (French)
   c. cantastorie 'lit. sing stories = street singer'   (Italian)
   d. limpa-chaminés 'lit. clean chimneys = chimney cleaner'
                                                    (Portuguese)
   e. fura-becuri 'lit. steal lightbulbs = tall person'   (Romanian)
                                        (Olsen (2015: 371–372))

Interestingly enough, Basciano and Melloni (2011), Basciano et al. (2011), Olsen (2015: 371–372), and Miller (2014: 54) notice the correlation between the productivity of VP-based agent nominals and that of agentive synthetic compounds, e.g. *truck-driver*. Basciano et al. (2011: 219) and Miller (2014: 54) suggest that VP-based agent nominals are unproductive in English because this language has the productive system of agentive synthetic compounding. On the other hand, Basciano and Melloni (2011: 28) and Olsen (2015: 371–372) observe that agentive synthetic compounds are unattested in Romance languages. On this observation, they point out that these languages exploit VP-based agent nominals to fill the gap left by the absence of agentive synthetic compounds.[9]

6. Summary

On the competition-theoretic assumption that English has no root compound, this appendix has pursued the lexicalization analysis of putative root compounds in English. Lexicalization is similar to compounding in that their outputs exhibit lexical properties, e.g. left-hand stress. But these two process-

---

[9] About VP-based agentive nominals, Ackema and Neeleman (2004: 161–162) observe that the verb-particle type is more productive than the verb-object type in English. According to their explanation, this contrast originates in the fact that English can derive synthetic compounds from verb-object but not from verb-particle combinations (e.g. **upcutter* (Ackema and Neeleman (2004: 162, fn. 18)) with a few exceptions. The present analysis suggests that the verb-particle type fills the gap left by the absence of synthetic compounds based on verb-particle combinations. This absence is an idiosyncrasy of English; the relevant type of synthetic compounds are attested in Dutch (e.g. *uitgever* 'lit. out-giver = publisher' (Ackema and Neeleman (2004: 71)).

es differ crucially as to whether they are responsible for structural realization. Since compounding is an option for morphological realization, its use as a default option is restricted to morphology-preferring languages. On the other hand, since lexicalization involves no structural realization, it is language-neutral. Therefore, this process is available even in syntax-preferring languages like English. Lexicalization consists of the listing of new items in the lexicon and the gradual loss of their internal structures. Characteristically, its outputs show non-uniformity in behavior. We have demonstrated that this behavioral non-uniformity can be found in a series of phrasal expressions that may be treated as compounds. Thus, they can be best analyzed as lexicalized phrases: they are in fact generated as syntactic phrases and may undergo accidental lexicalization to exhibit compound-like properties. Furthermore, it has been revealed that a certain type of N-N combination that looks like a synthetic compound can be best analyzed as an attributive phrase. While lexicalization can potentially occur in any language, it has cross-linguistic variations, depending on the morphosyntax of a given language.

References

Ackema, Peter and Ad Neeleman (2001) "Competition between Syntax and Morphology," *Optimality-Theoretic Syntax*, ed. by Géraldine Legendre, Jane Grimshaw and Sten Vikner, 29–60, MIT Press, Cambridge, MA.

Ackema, Peter and Ad Neeleman (2004) *Beyond Morphology: Interface Conditions on Word Formation*, Oxford University Press, Oxford.

Ackema, Peter and Ad Neeleman (2005) "Word-Formation in Optimality Theory," *Handbook of Word-Formation*, ed. by Pavol Štekauer and Rochelle Lieber, 285–313, Springer, Dordrecht.

Ackema, Peter and Ad Neeleman (2007) "Morphology ≠ Syntax," *The Oxford Handbook of Linguistic Interfaces*, ed. by Gillian Ramchand and Charles Reiss, 325–383, Oxford University Press, Oxford.

Ackema, Peter and Ad Neeleman (2010) "The Role of Syntax and Morphology in Compounding," *Cross-Disciplinary Issues in Compounding*, ed. by Sergio Scalise and Irene Vogel, 21–35, John Benjamins, Amsterdam and Philadelphia.

Ackerman, Farrell and Philip LeSourd (1997) "Toward a Lexical Representation of Phrasal Predicates," *Complex Predicates*, ed. by Alex Alsina, Joan Bresnan and Peter Sells, 67–106, CSLI Publications, Stanford.

Aikhenvald, Alexandra Y. (2004) *Evidentiality*, Oxford University Press, Oxford.

Alexiadou, Artemis, Liliane Haegeman and Melita Stavrou (2007) *Noun Phrase in the Generative Perspective*, Mouton de Gruyter, Berlin.

Allen, Margaret (1978) *Morphological Investigations*, Doctoral dissertation, University of Connecticut.

Alsina, Alex (1997) "A Theory of Complex Predicates: Evidence from Causatives in Bantu and Romance," *Complex Predicates*, ed. by Alex Alsina, Joan Bresnan and Peter Sells, 203–246, CSLI Publications, Stanford.

Anderson, Lloyd B. (1986) "Evidentials, Paths of Change, and Mental Maps: Typologically Regular Asymmetries," *Evidentiality: The Linguistic Coding of Epistemology*, ed. by Wallace Chafe and Johanna Nichols, 273–312, Ablex Publishing, Norwood, NJ.

Aoki, Haruo (1986) "Evidentials in Japanese," *Evidentiality: The Linguistic Coding of Epistemology*, ed. by Wallace Chafe and Johanna Nichols, 223–238, Ablex Publishing, Norwood, NJ.

Arcodia, Giorgio F., Nichola Grandi and Bernhard Wälchli (2010) "Coordination in Compounding," *Cross-Disciplinary Issues in Compounding*, ed. by Sergio Scalise and Irene Vogel, 177–197, John Benjamins, Amsterdam and Philadelphia.

Aronoff, Mark (1992) "Stems in Latin Verbal Morphology," *Morphology Now*, ed. by Mark Aronoff, 5–32, State University of New York Press, Albany.

Baker, Mark C. (1988) *Incorporation: A Theory of Grammatical Function Changing*, University of Chicago Press, Chicago.

Baker, Mark C. (1996) *The Polysynthesis Parameter*, Oxford University Press, Oxford.

Baker, Mark C. (2003a) *Lexical Categories: Verbs, Nouns, and Adjectives*, Cambridge University Press, Cambridge.

Baker, Mark C. (2003b) "'Verbal Adjectives' as Adjectives without Phi-features," *Proceedings of the 4th Tokyo Conference on Psycholinguistics*, ed. by Yukio Otsu, 1–22, Hituzi Syobo, Tokyo.

Baker, Mark C. (2008) "The Macroparameter in a Microparameteric World," *The Limits of Syntactic Variation*, ed. by Theresa Biberauer, 351–373, John Benjamins, Amsterdam and Philadelphia.

Baker, Mark C. (2010) "Formal Generative Typology," *The Oxford Handbook of Linguistic Analysis*, ed. by Bernd Heine and Heiko Narrog, 285–312, Oxford University Press, Oxford.

Basciano, Bianca and Chiara Melloni (2011) "VN and NV Compounds: A Comparative Overview," *Book of Abstracts the 44th Annual Meeting of the Societas Linguistica Europaea*, 28–29. <http://sle2011.cilap.es/downloads/book_abstracts.pdf>

Basciano, Bianca, Nancy Kula and Chiara Melloni (2011) "Modes of Compounding in Bantu, Romance and Chinese," *Rivista di Linguistica* 23, 203–249.

Bauer, Laurie (1983) *English Word-Formation*, Cambridge University Press, Cambridge.

Bauer, Laurie (1998) "When Is a Sequence of Two Nouns a Compound in English?," *English Language and Linguistics* 2, 65–86.

Bauer, Laurie (2003) *Introducing Linguistic Morphology*, 2nd ed., Edinburgh University Press, Edinburgh.

Bauer, Laurie (2008) "Dvandva," *Word Structure* 1, 1–20.

Beard, Robert (1995) *Lexeme-Morpheme Base Morphology: A General Theory of Inflection and Word Formation*, State University of New York Press, Albany.

Biber, Douglas, Stig Johansson, Geoffrey Leech, Susan Conrad and Edward Finegan (1999) *Longman Grammar of Spoken and Written English*, Longman, London.

Bloomfield, Leonard (1933) *Language*, Holt, Rinehart and Winston, New York.

References   149

Booij, Geert (2002a) "Constructional Idioms, Morphology, and the Dutch Lexicon," *Journal of Germanic Linguistics* 14, 301–329.

Booij, Geert (2002b) *The Morphology of Dutch*, Oxford University Press, Oxford.

Booij, Geert (2010) *Construction Morphology*, Oxford University Press, Oxford.

Borer, Hagit (1984) *Parametric Syntax: Case Studies in Semitic and Romance Languages*, Foris, Dordrecht.

Bowers, John (1993) "The Syntax of Predication," *Linguistic Inquiry* 24, 591–656.

Bresnan, Joan and Sam A. Mchombo (1995) "The Lexical Integrity Principle: Evidence from Bantu," *Natural Language and Linguistic Theory* 13, 181–254.

Brinton, Laurel J. and Elizabeth Closs Traugott (2005) *Lexicalization and Language Change*, Cambridge University Press, Cambridge.

Brown, Penelope and Stephen C. Levinson (1987) *Politeness: Some Universals in Language Usage*, Cambridge University Press, Cambridge.

Burstein, Jill C. (1992) *The Stress and Syntax of Compound Nominals*, Doctoral dissertation, City University of New York.

Ceccagno, Antonella and Bianca Basciano (2009) "Sino-Tibetan: Mandarin Chinese," *The Oxford Handbook of Compounding*, ed. by Rochelle Lieber and Pavol Štekauer, 465–478, Oxford University Press, Oxford.

Cheng, Lisa L. S. (1991) *On the Typology of Wh-Questions*, Doctoral dissertation, MIT.

Chomsky, Noam (1965) *Aspects of the Theory of Syntax*, MIT Press, Cambridge, MA.

Chomsky, Noam (1981) *Lectures on Government and Binding*, Foris, Dordrecht.

Chomsky, Noam (1982) *Some Concepts and Consequences of the Theory of Government and Binding*, MIT Press, Cambridge, MA.

Chomsky, Noam (1986) *Barriers*, MIT Press, Cambridge, MA.

Chomsky, Noam (1995) *The Minimalist Program*, MIT Press, Cambridge, MA.

Chomsky, Noam (2001a) "Beyond Explanatory Adequacy," *MIT Occasional Papers in Linguistics* 20, 1–28.

Chomsky, Noam (2001b) "Derivation by Phase," *Ken Hale: A Life in Language*, ed. by Michael Kenstowicz, 1–52, MIT Press, Cambridge, MA.

Chomsky, Noam (2010) "Some Simple Evo Theses," *The Evolution of Human Language: Biolinguistic Perspectives*, ed. by Richard K. Larson, Vivian Déprez and Hiroko Yamakido, 45–62, Cambridge University Press, Cambridge.

Cinque, Guglielmo (1999) *Adverbs and Functional Heads: A Cross-Linguistic Perspective*, Oxford University Press, Oxford.

Cinque, Guglielmo (2006) *Restructuring and Functional Heads*, Oxford University Press, Oxford.

Cinque, Guglielmo (2010) *The Syntax of Adjectives: A Comparative Study*, MIT Press, Cambridge, MA.

Cinque, Guglielmo and Luigi Rizzi (2010) "The Cartography of Syntactic Structures," *The Oxford Handbook of Linguistic Analysis*, ed. by Bernd Heine and Heiko Narrog, 51–65, Oxford University Press, Oxford.

Clark, Eve V. and Herbert H. Clark (1979) "When Nouns Surface as Verbs," *Language* 55, 767–811.

150 *A Study on Cross-Linguistic Variations in Realization Patterns*

Croft, William (2001) *Radical Construction Grammar: Syntactic Theory in Typological Perspective*, Oxford University Press, Oxford.

Di Sciullo, Anna-Maria and Edwin Williams (1987) *On the Definition of Word*, MIT Press, Cambridge, MA.

Dowty, David R. (1979) *Word Meaning and Montague Grammar: The Semantics of Verbs and Times in Generative Semantics and in Montague's PTQ*, D. Reidel, Dordrecht.

Embick, David (2010) *Localism versus Globalism in Morphology and Phonology*, MIT Press, Cambridge, MA.

Embick, David and Alec Marantz (2008) "Architecture and Blocking," *Linguistic Inquiry* 39, 1–53.

Endo, Yoshio (2009) "Hanashite to Kikite no Kaatogurafuii (The Cartography of the Speaker and the Addressee)," *Gengo Kenkyu* 136, 93–119.

Endo, Yoshio (2010) "Shujoshi no Kaatogurafuii (The Cartography of Sentence Final Particles)," *Togoron no Shintenkai to Nihongo Kenkyu: Meidai o Koete* (New Developments in Syntactic Theory and the Analysis of Japanese: Beyond Propositions), ed. by Nobuko Hasegawa, 67–94, Kaitakusha, Tokyo.

Endo, Yoshio (2014) *Nihongo Kaatogurafuii Josetsu* (Introduction to the Cartography of Japanese Syntactic Structures), Hituzi Syobo, Tokyo.

Escribano, José L. G. (2004) "Head-Final Effects and the Nature of Modification," *Journal of Linguistics* 40, 1–43.

Fabb, Nigel A. J. (1984) *Syntactic Affixation*, Doctoral dissertation, MIT.

Fradin, Bernard (2009) "IE, Romance: French," *The Oxford Handbook of Compounding*, ed. by Rochelle Lieber and Pavol Štekauer, 417–435, Oxford University Press, Oxford.

Giegerich, Heinz J. (2004) "Compound or Phrase? English Noun-Plus-Noun Constructions and the Stress Criterion," *English Language and Linguistics* 8, 1–24.

Giegerich, Heinz J. (2005) "Associative Adjectives in English and the Lexicon-Syntax Interface," *Journal of Linguistics* 41, 571–591.

Goldberg, Adele E. (1995) *Constructions: A Construction Grammar Approach to Argument Structure*, University of Chicago Press, Chicago.

Green, Georgia M. (1974) *Semantics and Syntactic Regularity*, Indiana University Press, Bloomington.

Grimshaw, Jane (1990) *Argument Structure*, MIT Press, Cambridge, MA.

Haegeman, Liliane (2006) "Argument Fronting in English, Romance CLLD and the Left Periphery," *Cross-Linguistic Research in Syntax and Semantics: Negation, Tense and Clausal Architecture*, ed. by Rafaella Zanuttini, Hector Campos, Elena Herburger and Paul Portner, 27–52, Georgetown University Press, Georgetown.

Haegeman, Liliane and Virginia Hill (2013) "The Syntacticization of Discourse," *Syntax and Its Limits*, ed. by Raffaella Folli, Christina Sevdali and Robert Truswell, 371–390, Oxford University Press, Oxford.

Hale, Kenneth and Samuel Jay Keyser (1993) "On Argument Structure and the Lexical

Expression of Syntactic Relations," *The View from Building 20: Essays in Linguistics in Honor of Sylvain Bromberger*, ed. by Kenneth Hale and Samuel Jay Keyser, 53‒109, MIT Press, Cambridge, MA.

Hale, Kenneth and Samuel Jay Keyser (1997) "On the Complex Nature of Simple Predicates," *Complex Predicates*, ed. by Alex Alsina, Joan Bresnan and Peter Sells, 29‒65, CSLI Publications, Stanford.

Hale, Kenneth and Samuel Jay Keyser (1998) "The Basic Elements of Argument Structure," *Papers from the UPenn / MIT Roundtable on Argument Structure and Aspect*, ed. by Heidi Harley, 73‒118.

Hale, Kenneth and Samuel Jay Keyser (2002) *Prolegomenon to a Theory of Argument Structure*, MIT Press, Cambridge, MA.

Hale, Kenneth and Samuel Jay Keyser (2005) "Aspect and the Syntax of Argument Structure," *The Syntax of Aspect: Deriving Thematic and Aspectual Interpretation*, ed. by Nomi Erteschik-Shir and Tova Rapoport, 11‒41, Oxford University Press, Oxford.

Halle, Morris and Alec Marantz (1993) "Distributed Morphology and the Pieces of Inflection," *The View from Building 20: Essays in Linguistics in Honor of Sylvain Bromberger*, ed. by Kenneth Hale and Samuel Jay Keyser, 111‒176, MIT Press, Cambridge, MA.

Harley, Heidi (2005) "How Do Verbs Get Their Names? Denominal Verbs, Manner Incorporation and the Ontology of Verb Roots in English," *The Syntax of Aspect: Deriving Thematic and Aspectual Interpretation*, ed. by Nomi Erteschik-Shir and Tova Rapoport, 42‒64, Oxford University Press, Oxford.

Hasegawa, Nobuko (1999) "The Syntax of Resultatives," *Linguistics: In Search of the Human Mind: A Festschrift for Kazuko Inoue*, ed. by Masatake Muraki and Enoch Iwamoto, 178‒208, Kaitakusha, Tokyo.

Hasegawa, Nobuko (2005) "The EPP Materialized First, Agree Later: Wh-Questions, Subjects and *Mo* 'Also'-Phrases," *Scientific Approaches to Language* 4, 33‒80, Kanda University of International Studies.

Haspelmath, Martin (2008) "Parametric versus Functional Explanations of Syntactic Universals," *The Limits of Syntactic Variation*, ed. by Theresa Biberauer, 75‒107, John Benjamins, Amsterdam and Philadelphia.

Haugen, Jason D. (2008) *Morphology at the Interfaces: Reduplication and Noun Incorporation in Uto-Aztecan*, John Benjamins, Amsterdam and Philadelphia.

Haugen, Jason D. (2009) "Hyponymous Objects and Late Insertion," *Lingua* 119, 242‒262.

Hawkins, Bruce W. (1993) "On Universality and Variability in the Semantics of Spatial Adpositions," *The Semantics of Prepositions: From Mental Processing to Natural Language Processing*, ed. by Cornelia Zelinsky-Wibbelt, 327‒349, Mouton de Gruyter, Berlin.

Hirose, Yukio (1995) "Direct and Indirect Speech as Quotations of Public and Private Expression," *Lingua* 95, 223‒238.

Hoshi, Koji (2002) "The Kaynean Analysis of Nominal Modification and Its Parametric

152   *A Study on Cross-Linguistic Variations in Realization Patterns*

Implications," *Language, Culture, and Communication* 29, 1–25, Keio University.

Hüning, Matthias (2010) "Adjective+Noun Constructions between Syntax and Word Formation in Dutch and German," *Cognitive Perspectives on Word Formation*, ed. by Alexander Onysko and Sascha Michel, 195–215, De Gruyter Mouton, Berlin.

Ikarashi, Keita (2013) "The Performative Clause *I Tell You*, Interpersonal Relationship, and Informational Superiority," *Tsukuba English Studies* 32, 116–126, University of Tsukuba.

Ikarashi, Keita (2014) "The Performative Clause *I Tell You* and the Speaker's Informational Superiority," ms., University of Tsukuba.

Imoto, Ryo (2009) "Nihongo Kekkakobun ni Okeru Gentei to Kyosei (Modification and Coercion in Japanese Resultative Constructions)," *Kekkakobun no Taiporojii* (The Typology of Resultative Constructions), ed. by Naoyuki Ono, 267–313, Hituzi Syobo, Tokyo.

Ito, Takane and Yoko Sugioka (2002) *Go no Shikumi to Gokeisei* (Word Structure and Word Formation), Kenkyusha, Tokyo.

Jackendoff, Ray (1997a) "Twistin' the Night Away," *Language* 73, 534–559.

Jackendoff, Ray (1997b) *The Architecture of the Language Faculty*, MIT Press, Cambridge, MA.

Jackendoff, Ray (2002a) "English Particle Constructions, the Lexicon, and the Autonomy of Syntax," *Verb-Particle Explorations*, ed. by Nicole Dehé, Ray Jackendoff, Andrew McIntyre and Silke Urban, 67–94, Mouton de Gruyter, Berlin.

Jackendoff, Ray (2002b) "What's in the Lexicon?," *Storage and Computation in the Language Faculty*, ed. by Sieb Nooteboom, Fred Weerman and Frank Wijnen, 23–58, Kluwer, Dordrecht.

Joos, Martin (1957) *Readings in Linguistics: The Development of Descriptive Linguistics in America since 1925*, American Council of Learned Societies, Washington.

Kageyama, Taro (1993) *Bunpo to Gokeisei* (Grammar and Word Formation), Hituzi Syobo, Tokyo.

Kageyama, Taro (1996) *Doshi Imiron: Gengo to Ninchi no Setten* (Verb Semantics: The Interface between Language and Cognition), Kurosio, Tokyo.

Kageyama, Taro (1997) "Denominal Verbs and Relative Salience in Lexical Conceptual Structure," *Verb Semantics and Syntactic Structure*, ed. by Taro Kageyama, 45–96, Kurosio, Tokyo.

Kageyama, Taro (2009) "Isolate: Japanese," *The Oxford Handbook of Compounding*, ed. by Rochelle Lieber and Pavol Štekauer, 512–526, Oxford University Press, Oxford.

Kageyama, Taro and Yoko Yumoto (1997) *Gokeisei to Gainenkozo* (Word Formation and Conceptual Structure), Kenkyusha, Tokyo.

Kamio, Akio (1994) "The Theory of Territory of Information: The Case of Japanese," *Journal of Pragmatics* 21, 67–100.

Kastovsky, Dieter (1982) *Wortbildung und Semantik*, Pädagogischer Verlag Schwann, Düsseldorf.

References 153

Kato, Kozo (2007) "Nihongo Kekkajutsugo wa Dosa Opushon Hyogen de Aru (Japanese Resultative Predicates Express Motion Option)," *Kekkakobun Kenkyu no Shinshiten* (A New Perspective of Resultative Construction Research), ed. by Naoyuki Ono, 217–248, Hituzi Syobo, Tokyo.

Kato, Kyoko and Taro Kageyama (1998) "Phrasal Compounds and Lexical Integrity," *English Linguistics* 15, 309–315.

Kayne, Richard S. (1994), *The Antisymmetry of Syntax*, MIT Press, Cambridge, MA.

Kechagias, Axitotis I. (2005) *Generating Words: Compounding in Modern Greek*, Master dissertation, University College London.

Kido, Yasuhito and Keiko Murasugi (2012) "Gengokakutoku no Kanten kara Saguru Shujoshi no Kino (On the Function of Sentence-Ending Markers in Child Japanese)," *Akademia: Bungaku · Gogakuhen* (Academia: Literature and Language) 92, 1–42, Nanzan University.

Kiparsky, Paul (1982) "Lexical Morphology and Phonology," *Linguistics in the Morning Calm: Selected Papers from SICOL-1981*, 3–91.

Kishimoto, Hideki (2001) "The Role of Lexical Meanings in Argument Encoding: Double Object Verbs in Japanese," *Gengo Kenkyu* 120, 35–65.

Kobayashi, Hideki (2004) *Gendai Nihongo no Kango Domeishi no Kenkyu* (A Study on Modern Sino-Japanese Verbal Nouns), Hituzi Syobo, Tokyo.

Kratzer, Angelika (1996) "Severing the External Argument from Its Verb," *Phrase Structure and the Lexicon*, ed. by Johan Rooryck and Laurie Zaring, 109–137, Kluwer, Dordrecht.

Kuno, Susumu (1973) *The Structure of the Japanese Language*, MIT Press, Cambridge, MA.

Kuroda, S.-Y. (1973) "Where Epistemology, Style, and Grammar Meet: A Case Study from Japanese," *A Festschrift for Morris Halle*, ed. by Stephen Anderson and Paul Kiparsky, 377–391, Holt, Rinehart and Winston, New York.

Lapointe, Steven (1980) *A Theory of Grammatical Agreement*, Doctoral dissertation, University of Massachusetts, Amherst. [Published by Garland, New York, 1985.]

Lees, Robert B. (1960) *The Grammar of English Nominalizations*, Mouton, The Hague.

Legendre, Géraldine (2001) "An Introduction to Optimality Theory in Syntax," *Optimality-Theoretic Syntax*, ed. by Géraldine Legendre, Jane Grimshaw and Sten Vikner, 1–27, MIT Press, Cambridge, MA.

Levi, Judith N. (1978) *The Syntax and Semantics of Complex Nominals*, Academic Press, New York.

Levin, Beth (1993) *English Verb Classes and Alternations: A Preliminary Investigation*, University of Chicago Press, Chicago.

Levin, Beth and Malka Rappaport Hovav (1995) *Unaccusativity: At the Syntax-Lexical Semantics Interface*, MIT Press, Cambridge, MA.

Li, Yafei (1993) "Structural Head and Aspectuality," *Language* 69, 480–504.

Liberman, Mark and Richard Sproat (1992) "The Stress and Structure of Modified Noun Phrases in English," *Lexical Matters*, ed. by Ivan A. Sag and Anna Szabolcsi, 131–181, CSLI Publications, Stanford.

Lieber, Rochelle (1988) "Phrasal Compounds in English and the Morphology-Syntax Interface," *CLS* 24, 202–222.

Lieber, Rochelle (1992) *Deconstructing Morphology: Word Formation in Syntactic Theory*, University of Chicago Press, Chicago.

Lieber, Rochelle and Pavol Štekauer (2009) "Introduction: Status and Definition of Compounding," *The Oxford Handbook of Compounding*, ed. by Rochelle Lieber and Pavol Štekauer, 3–18, Oxford University Press, Oxford.

Lindner, Susan Jean (1983) *A Lexico-Semantic Analysis of English Verb Particle Constructions with "Out" and "Up*,*"* Indiana University Linguistics Club.

Marantz, Alec (1984) *On the Nature of Grammatical Relations*, MIT Press, Cambridge, MA.

Marantz, Alec (1993) "Implications of Asymmetries in Double Object Constructions," *Theoretical Aspects of Bantu Grammar*, ed. by Sam A. Mchombo, 113–150, CSLI Publications, Stanford.

Marantz, Alec (1997) "No Escape from Syntax: Don't Try Morphological Analysis in the Privacy of Your Own Lexicon," *University of Pennsylvania Working Papers in Linguistics* 4, 201–225.

Marchand, Hans (1969) *The Categories and Types of Present-Day English Word-Formation: A Synchronic-Diachronic Approach*, 2nd ed., C. H. Beck'sche Verlagsbuchhandlung, München.

Mateu, Jaume (2012) "Conflation and Incorporation Processes in Resultative Constructions," *Telicity, Change, and State: A Cross-Categorial View of Event Structure*, ed. by Violeta Demonte and Louise McNally, 252–278, Oxford University Press, Oxford.

Mateu, Jaume (2014) "Argument Structure," *The Routledge Handbook of Syntax*, ed. by Andrew Carnie, Yosuke Sato and Daniel Siddiqi, 24–41, Routledge, New York.

McCarthy, John J. (2002) *A Thematic Guide to Optimality Theory*, Cambridge University Press, Cambridge.

McCarthy John J. and Alan Prince (1993) "Generalized Alignment," *Yearbook of Morphology 1993*, ed. by Geert Booij and Jaap van Marle, 79–153, Kluwer, Dordrecht.

Miller, Gary D. (2013) "On the History and Analysis of V-P Nouns," *Historical English Word-Formation and Semantics*, ed. by Jacek Fisiak and Magdalena Bator, 31–58, Peter Lang, Frankfurt.

Miller, Gary D. (2014) *English Lexicogenesis*, Oxford University Press, Oxford.

Mithun, Marianne (1986) "Evidential Diachrony in Northern Iroquoian," *Evidentiality: The Linguistic Coding of Epistemology*, ed. by Wallace Chafe and Johanna Nichols, 89–112, Ablex Publishing, Norwood, New Jersey.

Miyagawa, Shigeru (1989) *Structure and Case Marking in Japanese, Syntax and Semantics* 22, Academic Press, New York.

Miyakoshi, Koichi (2012) "'Kekkaku' no Jutsugosei to Fukushisei ni Tsuite: Kekka-hyogen no Teigi to Bunrui (On the Predicative and Adverbial Nature of 'Resultative Phrases': The Definition and Classification of Resultative Expressions)," paper presented at the symposium "Kekkahyogen o Megutte (On Resultative Expressions)," in the 84th Annual General Meeting of the English Literature Society of Japan.

Morita, Chigusa (2011) "Three Types of Direct Modification APs," *Linguistic Research* 27, 89–102, University of Tokyo.

Morita, Chigusa (2013) "The Morphology and Interpretations of Gradable Adjectives in Japanese," *English Linguistics* 30, 243–268.

Morita, Junya (1998) "Relationship between Morphology and Syntax in Core Grammar and the Periphery," *Kinjo Gakuin Daigaku Ronshu* (Treatises and Studies by the Faculty of Kinjo Gakuin University) 174, 387–409.

Morita, Junya (2003) "Mixture of Morphological and Syntactic Elements in English: A Dynamic View," *Empirical and Theoretical Investigations into Language: A Festschrift for Masaru Kajita*, ed. by Shuji Chiba et al. 419–434, Kaitakusha, Tokyo.

Murasugi, Keiko (2011) "Peripheral Particles in Early Child Japanese," paper presented at the 12th workshop of the International Research Project on Comparative Syntax at Nanzan University.

Nagano, Akiko (2008) *Conversion and Back-Formation in English*, Kaitakusha, Tokyo.

Nagano, Akiko (2010) "Subject Compounding and a Functional Change of the Derivational Suffix -*ing* in the History of English," *Variation and Change in English Grammar and Lexicon: Contemporary Approaches*, ed. by Robert A. Cloutier, Anne Marie Hamilton-Brehm and William A. Kretzschmar, Jr., 111–131, De Gruyter Mouton, Berlin.

Nagano, Akiko (2013) "Morphology of Direct Modification," *English Linguistics* 30, 111–150.

Nagano, Akiko and Masaharu Shimada (2010) "English [V-A]v Forms and the Interaction between Morphology and Syntax," *On-line Proceedings of the 7th Mediterranean Morphology Meeting*, ed. by Angela Ralli, Geert Booij, Sergio Scalise and Athanasios Karasimos, 78–97.

Nagano, Akiko and Masaharu Shimada (2014) "Morphological Theory and Orthography: *Kanji* as a Representation of Lexemes," *Journal of Linguistics* 50, 323–364.

Nagano, Akiko and Masaharu Shimada (2015) "Relational Adjectives (RAs) in Japanese and the RA vs. PP Debate," *On-line Proceedings of the 9th Mediterranean Morphology Meeting*, ed. by Jenny Audring, Nikos Koutsoukos, Francesca Masini and Ida Raffaelli, 105–133.

Namiki, Takayasu (1985) *Gokeisei* (Word Formation), Taishukan, Tokyo.

Napoli, Donna Jo (1992) "Secondary Resultative Predicates in Italian," *Journal of Linguistics* 28, 53–90.

Nespor, Marina and Irene Vogel (1986) *Prosodic Phonology*, Foris, Dordrecht.

Nishimaki, Kazuya (2014a) "On Morphosyntactic Competition in Nominal Modification," *JELS* 31, 95–101.

Nishimaki, Kazuya (2014b) "Competition Theory and Cross-Linguistic Variations,"

English Linguistics 31, 477–508.

Nishimaki, Kazuya (2016) "Cross-Linguistic Variations in Realization Patterns of Speech Act: A Competition-Theoretic Approach," *JELS* 33, 249–255.

Nishimaki, Kazuya (2018) "Possessional Adjectives as Transposed NPs," *JELS* 35, 287–293.

Nishiyama, Kunio (1998) "V-V Compounds as Serialization," *Journal of East Asian Linguistics* 7, 175–217.

Nishiyama, Kunio (1999) "Adjectives and the Copulas in Japanese," *Journal of East Asian Linguistics* 8, 183–222.

Nishiyama, Kunio (2005) "Verbs, Adjectives, and Pred: Review of Mark C. Baker, Lexical Categories," (Review Article: *Lexical Categories: Verbs, Nouns, and Adjectives*, by Mark C. Baker, Cambridge University Press, Cambridge, 2003,) *English Linguistics* 22, 133–161.

Nitta, Yoshio (2002) *Fukushiteki Hyogen no Shoso* (Aspects of Adverbials), Kurosio, Tokyo.

Oishi, Tsuyoshi (1988) *Keitairon* (Morphology), Kaitakusha,Tokyo.

Okura, Naoko (2011) "Juekikobun to, Kinohanchu toshiteno *Ageru* (Benefactive Constructions, and *Ageru* 'Give' as Functional Category)," *70 Nendai Seiseibunpo Saininshiki: Nihongo Kenkyu no Chihei* (A New Understanding of 70s' Generative Grammar: The Horizon of Japanese Linguistics), ed. by Nobuko Hasegawa, 231–252, Kaitakusha,Tokyo.

Olsen, Susan (2000) "Composition," *Morphology: An International Handbook on Inflection and Word-Formation*, ed. by Geert Booij, Christian Lehmann and Joachim Mugdan, 897–916, Walter de Gruyter, Berlin.

Olsen, Susan (2001) "Copulative Compounds: A Closer Look at the Interface between Syntax and Morphology," *Yearbook of Morphology 2000*, ed. by Geert Booij and Jaap van Marle, 279–320, Kluwer, Dordrecht.

Olsen, Susan (2015) "Composition," *Word-Formation: An International Handbook of the Languages of Europe* 1, ed. by Peter O. Müller, Ingeborg Ohnheiser, Susan Olsen and Franz Rainer, 364–386, De Gruyter Mouton, Berlin.

Ono, Naoyuki (2007) "Kekkakobun o Meguru Mondai (Issues concerning Resultative Constructions)," *Kekkakobun Kenkyu no Shinshiten* (A New Perspective of Resultative Construction Research), ed. by Naoyuki Ono, 1–31, Hituzi Syobo, Tokyo.

Oshita, Hiroyuki (1995) "Compounds: A View from Suffixation and A-Structure Alternation," *Yearbook of Morphology 1994*, ed. by Geert Booij and Jaap van Marle, 179–205, Kluwer, Dordrecht.

Perlmutter, David (1978) "Impersonal Passives and the Unaccusative Hypothesis," *BLS* 4, 157–190.

Pesetsky, David (1995) *Zero Syntax: Experiencers and Cascades*, MIT Press, Cambridge, MA.

Plag, Ingo (2003) *Word-Formation in English*, Cambridge University Press, Cambridge.

Poser, William J. (1992) "Blocking of Phrasal Constructions by Lexical Items," *Lexical*

Matters, ed. by Ivan A. Sag and Anna Szabolcsi, 111‒130, CSLI Publications, Stanford.

Prince, Alan and Paul Smolensky (1993), *Optimality Theory: Constraint Interaction in Generative Grammar*. Technical Report TR-2, Center for Cognitive Science, Rutgers University, New Brunswick, N.J., and Technical Report CU-CS-696-93, Department of Computer Science, University of Colorado, Boulder. [Published by Blackwell, Malden, MA, 2004.]

Pylkkänen, Liina (2008) *Introducing Arguments*, MIT Press, Cambridge, MA.

Quirk, Randolph, Sidney Greenbaum, Geoffrey Leech and Jan Svartvik (1985) *A Comprehensive Grammar of the English Language*, Longman, London.

Ralli, Angela (1992) "Compounds in Modern Greek," *Rivista di Linguistica* 4, 143‒147.

Ralli, Angela (2008) "Compound Markers and Parametric Variation," *Sprachtypologie und Universalienforschung* 61, 19‒38.

Ralli, Angela (2009) "IE, Hellenic: Modern Greek," *The Oxford Handbook of Compounding*, ed. by Rochelle Lieber and Pavol Štekauer, 453‒463, Oxford University Press, Oxford.

Rizzi, Luigi (1997) "The Fine Structure of the Left-Periphery," *Elements of Grammar: A Handbook of Generative Syntax*, ed. by Liliane Haegeman, 281‒337, Kluwer, Dordrecht.

Roeper, Thomas (1987) "Implicit Arguments and the Head-Complement Relation," *Linguistic Inquiry* 18, 267‒310.

Roeper, Thomas and Muffy E. A. Siegel (1978) "A Lexical Transformation for Verbal Compounds," *Linguistic Inquiry* 9, 199‒260.

Rosenbach, Anette (2007) "Emerging Variation: Determiner Genitives and Noun Modifiers in English," *English Language and Linguistics* 11, 143‒189.

Rosenbach, Anette (2010) "How Synchronic Gradience Makes Sense in the Light of Language Change (and Vice Versa)," *Gradience, Gradualness and Grammaticalization*, ed. by Elizabeth Closs Traugott and Graeme Trousdale, 149‒179, John Benjamins, Amsterdam and Philadelphia.

Sadler, Louisa and Douglas J. Arnold (1994) "Prenominal Adjectives and the Phrasal / Lexical Distinction," *Journal of Linguistics* 30, 187‒226.

Saito, Mamoru (2012) "Sentence Types and the Japanese Right Periphery," *Discourse and Grammar: From Sentence Types to Lexical Categories*, ed. by Günther Grewendorf and Thomas Ede Zimmermann, 147‒175, De Gruyter Mouton, Berlin.

Saito, Mamoru and Hiroto Hoshi (2000) "The Japanese Light Verb Construction and the Minimalist Program," *Step by Step: Essays on Minimalist Syntax in Honor of Howard Lasnik*, ed. by Roger Martin, David Michaels and Juan Uriagereka, 261‒298, MIT Press, Cambridge, MA.

Scalise, Sergio and Antonio Fábregas (2010) "The Head in Compounding," *Cross-Disciplinary Issues in Compounding*, ed. by Sergio Scalise and Irene Vogel, 109‒126, John Benjamins, Amsterdam and Philadelphia.

Scott, Gary-John (2002) "Stacked Adjectival Modification and the Structure of

Nominal Phrases," *Functional Structure in DP and IP*, ed. by Guglielmo Cinque, 91–120, Oxford University Press, Oxford.

Selkirk, Elisabeth O. (1982) *The Syntax of Words*, MIT Press, Cambridge, MA.

Shibatani, Masayoshi (1990) *The Languages of Japan*, Cambridge University Press, Cambridge.

Shibatani, Masayoshi and Taro Kageyama (1988) "Word Formation in a Modular Theory of Grammar: Postsyntactic Compounds in Japanese," *Language* 64, 451–484.

Shimada, Masaharu (2012) "Three Types of Coordinated Compounds: Comparison between Western and Asian Languages," paper presented at Universals and Typology in Word-Formation II held at Šafárik University.

Shimada, Masaharu (2013) "Coordinated Compounds: Comparison between English and Japanese," *SKASE Journal of Theoretical Linguistics* 10, 77–96.

Shimamura, Reiko (1986) "Lexicalization of Syntactic Phrases," *English Linguistics* 3, 20–37.

Shimamura, Reiko (1999) "Lexicalization of Syntactic Phrases: The Case of Genitive Compounds like *Woman's Magazine*," *Grant-in-Aid for COE Research Report (3): Researching and Verifying an Advanced Theory of Human Language*, ed. by Kazuko Inoue, 277–300, Kanda University of International Studies.

Shimamura, Reiko (2003) "On Lexicalized Phrases," *Empirical and Theoretical Investigations into Language: A Festschrift for Masaru Kajita*, ed. by Shuji Chiba et al., 631–646, Kaitakusha, Tokyo.

Shimamura, Reiko (2005) "Ku no Goika ni Tsuite: Eigo no Meishi Zeni Shushoku Hyogen o Chushin ni (On the Lexicalization of Phrases: With Special Reference to Prenominal Modifiers in English)," *Gendai Keitairon no Choryu* (The Current of Contemporary Morphology), ed. by Tsuyoshi Oishi, Tetsuo Nishihara and Youji Toyoshima, 55–73, Kurosio, Tokyo.

Shimamura, Reiko (2007) "The Adjective-Noun Expression within the Word Revisited: The Boundary between Phrase and Word," *Language Beyond: A Festschrift for Hiroshi Yonekura on the Occasion of His 65th Birthday*, ed. by Mayumi Sawada, Larry Walker and Shizuya Tara, 367–395, Eichosha, Tokyo.

Shimamura, Reiko (2014) *Go to Ku to Nazukekino: Nichieigo no "Keiyoshi + Meishi" Kei o Chushin ni* (Words, Phrases, and Naming Function: With Special Reference to "Adjective + Noun" Constructions in English and Japanese), Kaitakusha, Tokyo.

Shizawa, Takashi (2015a) "The Rhetorical Effect of Locative Inversion Constructions from the Perspective of the Three-Tier Model of Language Use," *English Linguistics* 32, 156–176.

Shizawa, Takashi (2015b) "'Bashotochikobun' no Nichiei Taisho Kenkyu: Gojun to Jokyohaku no Moodo (A Comparative Study of 'Locative Inversion Construction' between English and Japanese: Word Order and the Mode of Situation Construal)," *Proceedings of the 67th Annual Meeting of the Tohoku Branch of the English Literary Society of Japan*, 128–129.

Siegel, Muffy E. A. (1976) *Capturing the Adjective*, Doctoral dissertation, University of Massachusetts.

Snyder, William (1995) *Language Acquisition and Language Variation: The Role of Morphology*, Doctoral dissertation, MIT.

Snyder, William (2001) "On the Nature of Syntactic Variation: Evidence from Complex Predicates and Complex Word-Formation," *Language* 77, 324–342.

Snyder, William (2012) "Parameter Theory and Motion Predicates," *Telicity, Change, and State: A Cross-Categorial View of Event Structure*, ed. by Violeta Demonte and Louise McNally, 277–299, Oxford University Press, Oxford.

Speas, Peggy and Carol L. Tenny (2003) "Configurational Properties of Point of View Roles," *Asymmetry in Grammar* I, ed. by Anna-Maria Di Sciullo, 315–344, John Benjamins, Amsterdam and Philadelphia.

Spencer, Andrew (2003) "Does English Have Productive Compounding," *Topics in Morphology*, ed. by Geert Booij, Janet DeCesaris, Angela Ralli and Sergio Scalise, 329–341, IULA, Barcelona.

Sportiche, Dominique (1992) "Clitic Constructions," ms., UCLA.

Sproat, Richard W. (1985) *On Deriving the Lexicon*, Doctoral dissertation, MIT.

Sproat, Richard W. (1993) "Morphological Non-separation Revisited: A Review of R. Lieber's *Deconstructing Morphology*," (Review Article: *Deconstructing Morphology: Word Formation in Syntactic Theory*, by Rochelle Lieber, University of Chicago Press, Chicago, 1992,) *Yearbook of Morphology 1992*, ed. by Geert Booij and Jaap van Marle, 235–258, Springer, Dordrecht.

Sproat, Richard and Chilin Shih (1991) "The Cross-Linguistic Distribution of Adjective Ordering Restrictions," *Interdisciplinary Approaches to Language: Essays in Honor of S.-Y. Kuroda*, ed. by Carol Georgopoulos and Roberta Ishihara, 565–593, Kluwer, Dordrecht.

Stubbs, Michael (1983) *Discourse Analysis: The Sociolinguistic Analysis of Natural Language*, University of Chicago Press, Chicago.

Sugioka, Yoko and Hideki Kobayashi (2001) "Meishi+Doshi no Fukugogo (Compounds of Nouns+Verbs)," *Nichiei Taisho Doshi no Imi to Kobun* (A Comparative Study of English and Japanese Semantics and Constructions of Verbs), ed. by Taro Kageyama, 242–268, Taishukan, Tokyo.

Svenonius, Peter (2006) "The Emergence of Axial Parts," *Nordlyd: Tromsø Working Papers in Linguistics* 33, 49–77.

Takahashi, Hideya (2013a) "Nihongo no 'Haseiteki' Kekkakobun ni Okeru Asupekuto Gentei (Aspectual Modification in Japanese 'Derived' Resultatives)," paper at Morphology and Lexicon Forum 2013 at Keio University.

Takahashi, Hideya (2013b) "Nihongo ni Okeru 'Haseiteki' Kekkakobun no Keitaitogoron ni Tsuite (A Morphosyntactic Approach to Resultatives in Japanese and Labeling Algorithm in Minimalist Syntax)," *Liberal Arts* 7, 1–20, Iwate Prefectural University.

Talmy, Leonard (1985) "Lexicalization Patterns: Semantic Structure in Lexical Forms," *Language Typology and Syntactic Description* III: *Grammatical Categories and the Lexicon*, ed. by Timothy Shopen, 57–149, Cambridge University Press,

160   *A Study on Cross-Linguistic Variations in Realization Patterns*

Cambridge.

Talmy, Leonard (1991) "Path to Realization: A Typology of Event Conflation," *BLS* 17, 480–519.

Talmy, Leonard (2000) *Typology and Process in Concept Structuring*, MIT Press, Cambridge, MA.

Taylor, John R. (1996) *Possessives in English: An Exploration in Cognitive Grammar*, Oxford University Press, Oxford.

ten Hacken, Pius (1994) *Defining Morphology: A Principled Approach to Determining the Boundaries of Compounding, Derivation and Inflection*, Georg Olms, Hildesheim.

Tenny, Carol L. (1994) *Aspectual Roles and the Syntax-Semantics Interface*, Kluwer, Dordrecht.

Tenny, Carol L. (2006) "Evidentiality, Experiencers, and the Syntax of Sentience in Japanese," *Journal of East Asian Linguistics* 15, 245–288.

Traugott, Elizabeth Closs (1994) "Grammaticalization and Lexicalization," *The Encyclopedia of Language and Linguistics* III, ed. by R. E. Asher and J. M. Y. Simpson, 1481–1486, Pergamon Press, Oxford and Tokyo.

Travis, Lisa (1984) *Parameters and Effects of Word Order Variation*, Doctoral dissertation, MIT.

Tsujimura, Natsuko (2007) *An Introduction to Japanese Linguistics*, 2nd ed., Blackwell, Malden, MA.

Tsukamoto, Hideki (2012) *Keitairon to Togoron no Sogosayo: Nihongo to Chosengo no Taisho Gengogakuteki Kenkyu* (The Interaction between Morphology and Syntax: A Comparative Study of Japanese and Korean), Hituzi Syobo, Tokyo.

Uyeno, Tazuko (1971) *A Study of Japanese Modality: A Performative Analysis of Sentence Particles*, Doctoral dissertation, University of Michigan.

Washio, Ryuichi (1997) "Resultatives, Compositionality, and Language Variation," *Journal of East Asian Linguistics* 6, 1–49.

Watanabe, Akira (2012) "Direct Modification in Japanese," *Linguistic Inquiry* 43, 504–513.

Wechsler, Stephen (2005) "Resultatives under the 'Event-Argument Homomorphism' Model of Telicity," *The Syntax of Aspect: Deriving Thematic and Aspectual Interpretation*, ed. by Nomi Erteschik-Shir and Tova Rapoport, 255–273, Oxford University Press, Oxford.

Williams, Edwin (1981) "On the Notions 'Lexically Related' and 'Head of a Word'," *Linguistic Inquiry* 12, 245–274.

Williams, Edwin (1982) "Another Argument That Passive Is Transformational," *Linguistic Inquiry* 13, 160–163.

Yamakido, Hiroko (2005) *The Nature of Adjectival Inflection in Japanese*, Doctoral dissertation, Stony Brook University.

Yasuhara, Masaki and Kazuya Nishimaki (2015) "Double Object Constructions in Japanese: A Competition-Theoretic Approach," *Proceedings of the 17th Seoul International Conference on Generative Grammar*, 584–596.

Yasuhara, Masaki and Kazuya Nishimaki (2017) "A Unified Account of Directed Motion Constructions in English and Japanese," *Proceedings of the 12th Workshop on Altaic Formal Linguistics*, ed. by Leyla Zidani-Eroğlu, Matthew Ciscel and Elena Koulidobrova, 321–332.

Yoda, Yusuke (2010) "Sore wa Hontoni Toikozo? (Is It Really a Coordinated Structure?)," *Nihongo Nihonbunka Kenkyu* (Studies in Japanese Language and Culture) 60, 65–75, Osaka University.

Zubizarreta, Maria Luisa and Eunjeong Oh (2007) *On the Syntactic Composition of Manner and Motion*, MIT Press, Cambridge, MA.

Zwanenburg, Wiecher (1992) "Compounding in French," *Rivista di Linguistica* 4, 221–240.

CORPORA

Balanced Corpus of Contemporary Written Japanese Chunagon (Chunagon Corpus) <https://chunagon.ninjal.ac.jp/search>

British National Corpus (BNC) <http://bnc.jkn21.com/>

DICTIONARIES

Cambridge English Pronouncing Dictionary (Cambridge) (15th ed.), Cambridge University Press, Cambridge.

Collins COBUILD Dictionary on CD-ROM (COBUILD), Harper Collins, London.

Kenkyusha's New Japanese-English Dictionary (Kenkyusha's Dictionary) (4th ed.), Kenkyusha, Tokyo.

Longman Pronunciation Dictionary (Longman), Longman, London.

Oxford English Dictionary Online (OED) <http://www.oed.com/>

Sanseido's Shinmeikai Japanese Accent Dictionary (Sanseido's Dictionary) (2nd ed.), Sanseido, Tokyo.

Taishukan's Unabridged Genius English-Japanese Dictionary (Taishukan's Dictionary), Taishukan, Tokyo.

Index

A

adposition   25, 102, 112–113, 115, 119

Appl(icative)   103–106

B

blocking   9, 27–28, 32

bound morpheme   2fn, 6, 25, 40, 66fn, 83, 86, 88fn, 91

C

clustering effect   23, 31

Coanalysis   89

(morphology-syntax) competition   1–2, 5, 7, 9–16, 15fn–17fn, 18–22, 20fn, 26–29, 31–34, 39, 41, 44, 47, 49–50, 52, 53fn, 55, 55fn, 57, 61, 64, 67, 71–72, 80, 82, 86, 92, 97, 101, 106fn, 116–117, 120–121, 123, 125, 131, 144

Competition Theory   1–5, 7, 9–10, 12, 14–15, 18–20, 22–24, 26–27, 31–33, 38, 41, 43–44, 46–50, 52, 53fn, 55, 57–58, 60–61, 65, 71, 76, 81–82, 86, 89, 91–93, 97–98, 101–102, 108–109, 116–117, 120–121, 123, 126, 138

competitor   16, 22, 27, 54fn

compound

A-N compound   2, 39, 41–44, 42fn–43fn, 45fn, 48, 65, 76, 81–82, 117, 122, 127, 143

appositional compound   72–76, 80–81, 81fn

co-participant compound   23, 73–75

genitive compound   132–133

N-N compound   19, 54fn–55fn, 80, 122, 127, 143

N-V compound   15, 17fn, 108, 112fn

phrasal compound   135–136

resultative V-V compound (RVVC)   62–65, 67, 109–110, 110fn

root compound   18–19, 31, 81, 123–124, 126–127, 131–132, 136, 144

synthetic compound   16, 18–22, 30, 123–124, 127, 137–141, 139fn, 142fn, 144–145, 144fn

verbal compound   16–18, 21–22, 26, 30, 50, 94

V-V compound   5–6, 58–59, 61–62, 68, 70, 97fn, 122

163

compounding
  A-N compounding   43, 52, 55fn
  synthetic compounding   144
confirmation to the hearer   25, 119
conflation   7, 53fn, 92–99, 101–104, 106–
  110, 113–116, 119, 121
construction
  ageru construction   102–106
  body part *off* construction (BPOC)   24,
    68, 70–71, 118
  double object construction (DOC)   25,
    102–103, 119
  resultative construction   5–6, 24, 58–62,
    64fn, 65, 67–68, 71, 102, 108, 118
  'time'-*away* construction   24, 68, 70–
    71, 118
  unergative construction   25, 102, 119
  verb particle construction (VPC)   24,
    68, 70–71, 118, 135
(N-to-V) conversion   6–7, 93, 100–101,
  134fn
coordination   24, 50, 58, 64fn, 78–79,
  79fn, 118, 137
cross-linguistic variation   2–3, 5, 7, 13,
  24, 30–31, 35, 38, 41, 57–58, 64,
  64fn, 72, 76, 84, 91, 93, 106, 117,
  121fn, 124, 142–143, 145

D

(non-)default   10, 18, 23, 26–27, 29, 31,
  57, 110fn, 116, 120–121, 125, 145
direct merger   21, 40fn, 79, 82
(in)direct modifier   36, 38, 39fn, 51–52,
  54, 52fn–55fn, 101
discourse marker   6, 58, 82, 89
Distributed Morphology   142fn
dvandva   71–79, 77fn, 79fn, 81–82, 117,
  122

E

Elsewhere Condition   9

embedded productivity   22, 26, 49
-*er*   13, 19, 21–22, 26, 30, 50, 123, 138,
  141
event control   138–139, 139fn
evidentiality   88–89, 88fn, 119
Extended Projection Principle   28
externalization   3, 13, 117

F

form
  bound form   6, 25–26, 40, 53fn, 55fn,
    58, 82, 85–86, 92, 116, 119
  complex form   25–26, 102, 113, 116,
    119
  free form   6, 25–26, 40, 53fn, 58, 82–
    83, 85–86, 88–89, 91–92, 116, 119
  morphologically-realized form   18, 24,
    39, 41, 49, 64, 76, 80, 82, 98, 117,
    120, 123
  realization form   1, 4, 6, 15, 20, 27, 50,
    58, 64, 64fn, 91, 97, 117, 125–126
  simplex form   25–26, 102, 113–114,
    116, 119
  syntactically-realized form   24, 43, 50,
    64, 120, 131
functional head   20fn, 38, 66–67, 82, 103,
  106, 112

G

genitive NP   51–54, 51fn, 54fn–55fn, 101,
  115

H

head movement   7, 58, 65, 67, 92–93, 98,
  100–102, 104, 108–109, 110fn
Head Movement Constraint   67
hearsay   88, 119

I

(noun) incorporation   7, 53fn, 92–103,
  105–108, 110–116, 110fn, 112fn, 119,
  121
-*ing*   19, 22, 26, 123–124, 138, 141

interrogative 25, 25fn, 87, 87fn, 119
(non-)intersective 36–37, 37fn, 39, 44–46,
    81–82
IS A Condition 73–74, 76, 80

L

language
    conflating language 93, 98
    incorporating language 93–94, 96, 98
    polysynthetic language 17, 88fn, 94,
        100–101, 108, 112, 115, 121
    stem-based language 92, 122
    word-based language 92
Late Insertion 12
lexical category 35, 37–38, 77, 125
Lexical Integrity Principle (LIP) 3, 5,
    44fn, 50, 105–107, 127, 131fn, 136
lexicalization 19–20, 43, 81, 123–127,
    130–137, 131fn, 142–145
lexicon 11–14, 19, 46, 79, 81, 86, 89, 91,
    124–125, 131, 131fn, 134, 142, 145

M

(un)marked 1, 4, 9, 27, 35, 49, 101, 110,
    115, 120
Minimalist Program 3, 14, 98, 106
minimizing
    morphological-complexity minimiz-
        ing 26, 97–98, 121
    syntactic-complexity minimizing 26,
        98, 116, 121
modification
    (in)direct modification 35–41, 43–46,
        47fn, 49–50, 52, 55, 54fn–55fn, 58,
        64, 82, 117
    nominal modification 2–3, 5–7, 24, 33–
        35, 37, 39, 45–48, 54fn, 55, 57, 71,
        76, 118
morphology 1, 3–4, 9–20, 17fn, 22–24,
    26–27, 31–32, 41, 44, 48–49, 52,
    53fn, 55, 57–58, 61, 71, 76, 84, 86,

88fn, 91–93, 96–98, 101–102, 104,
    106, 108, 110, 115–117, 120–123,
    123fn, 125, 132, 145
morphology-preferring (language) 12–15,
    17–18, 17fn, 20, 23–24, 26, 31–32,
    41, 52, 53fn, 57–58, 61, 71, 76, 86,
    88fn, 91–93, 96–98, 101–102, 104,
    106, 108, 110, 115–116, 120–122,
    125, 145

N

naming 46–49, 46fn–47fn, 72, 141–142

O

one-sided information giving 25, 83, 119
Optimality Theory (OT) 26–28, 30–32
(c)overt 23fn, 84, 96, 101, 105–108,
    106fn, 113–114

P

parameter
    macroparameter 4, 23, 31, 41, 57, 64fn,
        102, 116, 120
    microparameter 4, 64fn
    Polysynthesis Parameter 101–102
PF 11–15, 31, 80, 98
Possessional adjective 50, 141fn
Pred(icate) 37, 66–67, 82, 110–111, 111fn
Principles-and-Parameters approach 3
Proper Head Movement Generalization
    (PHMG) 67, 112–113

R

random (process) 4, 126, 130
realization
    morphological realization 14–18, 20,
        22–24, 26, 29, 31, 40fn, 48–50, 52,
        57, 65, 86, 116–117, 120–121, 123,
        145
    structural realization 5, 10–12, 14, 20,
        27, 55, 58, 86, 125–126, 142, 145
    syntactic realization 14–17, 23, 26, 29–
        30, 48–50, 52, 54, 57–58, 116–117,

120–121

realization pattern 2, 4–6, 27, 29, 31, 33–35, 47–49, 57–58, 65, 67, 82, 91, 106, 106fn, 108, 118, 120

relational adjective (RAdj) 51–54, 52fn–53fn, 101

relative clause 37, 41, 45

representation 11–12, 72, 84, 86, 89–90

Representational Modularity (Model) 10–13, 31, 79, 89

request for hearer's agreement 25, 119

resultative

strong resultative 60–65, 64fn, 68, 108–109, 117, 122

weak resultative 60–61, 65–67, 108, 110–112, 111fn, 122

resultative predicate 38fn, 59–60, 62–63, 64fn, 65, 67, 108, 111fn

Righthand Head Rule (RHR) 132–133, 143

rule-governed (process) 126, 128, 132–133, 143

S

sentence-final particle (SFP) 83, 85–91, 85fn, 87fn

Separation Hypothesis 12

speech act 6, 25, 58, 82–83, 85–86, 85fn, 89–90, 119

Split CP hypothesis 83

structure

argument structure 138–139, 139fn, 141–142, 142fn

asymmetrical structure 6, 71, 82

coordinated structure 6, 58, 71–72, 74, 76–79

endocentric structure 133–134

Genuine Coordinate Structure 78–79,

82

Pseudo Coordinate Structure 78

syntactic opacity 3, 136

syntax 1–4, 9–20, 17fn, 23–24, 26–27, 31–32, 40–41, 48, 50, 55, 57–58, 62, 71, 76, 79, 86, 91–93, 95–98, 97fn, 101–102, 104, 106, 108, 110, 115, 117, 120–123, 125, 132, 140fn, 141, 145

syntax-preferring (language) 12–15, 17–18, 20, 23–24, 26, 31–32, 41, 48, 50, 55, 57–58, 71, 76, 79, 86, 91–93, 96–98, 97fn, 101–102, 104, 106, 108, 110, 115, 120–123, 125, 145

T

Temporal Iconicity Condition (TIC) 62, 110fn

U

(non-)uniformity 126–128, 133, 137, 143, 145

Uniformity Principle 3, 13, 91

Unique Path Constraint 62

Universal Grammar (UG) 26–27, 29

V

verb

activity verb 60–62, 70, 110

change-of-state verb 59–60, 62, 110

light verb 93, 107–108

manner-of-speaking verb 94, 96

unergative verb 6–7, 93, 96, 106

verbal N-N combination 137–141

violable principles or constraints 27–28, 32

W

word formation 6–7, 16, 22, 38fn, 92–93, 95, 124–125, 139

A Study on Cross-Linguistic Variations in Realization
Patterns: New Proposals Based on Competition Theory

著作者　西 牧 和 也
発行者　武 村 哲 司
印刷所　日之出印刷株式会社

2018 年 10 月 23 日　第 1 版第 1 刷発行ⓒ

発行所　　株式会社　開 拓 社

〒113-0023 東京都文京区向丘 1-5-2
電話　(03) 5842-8900 (代表)
振替　00160-8-39587
http://www.kaitakusha.co.jp

JCOPY ＜出版者著作権管理機構 委託出版物＞

ISBN978-4-7589-2261-6　C3080

本書の無断複製は，著作権法上での例外を除き禁じられています．複製される場合は，そのつど事前に，出版者著作権管理機構（電話 03-3513-6969，FAX 03-3513-6979，e-mail: info@jcopy.or.jp）の許諾を得てください．